THE
MOUNT ASPIRING
REGION

a guide for mountaineers

Revised and enlarged from
Graham Bishop's original guidebook

Allan Uren
and Mark Watson

Published by the New Zealand Alpine Club 2001

ABOUT THE AUTHORS

ALLAN UREN moved to Wanaka in 1977 and his proximity to the Aspiring region germinated the mountaineering seed. This seed had lain dormant during his childhood, living under the shadow of the Takitimu Mountains in Southland. He has climbed in Alaska and elsewhere in the USA but prefers the mountains of home. His ways of supporting his climbing habit are varied—he has been a painter and decorator, abseil access technician, kitchen-hand, ski-patroller and more recently a freelance writer. He has had articles published in *The Climber*, *New Zealand Alpine Journal*, *New Zealand Geographic*, *Wilderness* and *Adventure* magazines. He currently lives, loves and climbs from a new base in Fox Glacier.

MARK WATSON lives in Christchurch and has been climbing since 1987. At the time this guide was being completed he was also working as the Editor of the New Zealand Alpine Club's quarterly magazine; *The Climber*. His enthusiasm for the outdoors was fostered at a young age in Wellington's stormy Tararua Ranges and the volcanoes of the Central North Island. He loves climbing of all types but is presently more likely to be found among the boulders and crags of the Castle Hill Basin, although sporadic forays into the Southern Alps do occur.

© New Zealand Alpine Club 2001
PO Box 786, Christchurch

Distribution enquiries:
New Zealand Alpine Club Publications
Ph (03)377-7595 l Fax (03)377-7594
E-mail publications@alpineclub.org.nz

This book is the successor to:
Graham Bishop's *The Mount Aspiring Region* 1974
Reprinted 1976
Reprinted with minor revision, 1981
Reprinted with further revision and new illustrations, 1989
Reprinted 1999
Completely revised and expanded 2001, Allan Uren and Mark Watson
Reprinted with minor revision 2004

Edited, revised and new sections written by Allan Uren
Co-edited, designed and typeset by Mark Watson

Set in Adobe Garamond and Frutiger
Printed by Saxon Print, Christchurch

ISBN 0-9597630-9-0

Front cover: The north side of Mount Aspiring. The popular North West Ridge route runs from centre to right. *Colin Monteath/Hedgehog House.*

"This is the way, walk ye in it"
—*Isaiah* XXXV

On the Bonar Glacier, descending Pope's Nose during winter.
Duncan Ritchie.

Acknowledgements

We'd like to acknowledge Graham Bishop's original efforts in putting the original information together for this guide; he must have laboured long and hard. Huge thanks go out to: Duncan Ritchie for the use of his slides and the bits of his brain picked by Al to find the good rock in the Aspiring region, Colin Monteath/Hedgehog House and Geoff Wayatt for the stunning pictures, Richard Thomson for researching the Northern section and Hana Black for proof-reading and other input. Acknowledgement is also due to Stu Allan, Geoff Spearpoint, Ross Cullen, Geoff Wayatt and Graham Bishop for commenting on the drafts.

Thanks to all the people we've wandered into the hills with. Yeeehaa!

This book is dedicated to Phil Penney.

Allan Uren and Mark Watson 2001.

CONTENTS

Aspiring

And she lies breathing

Sighing in the infancy her eyes watch gracefully

Scanning insignificant forms…

Mother of the hills

The breath of which she breathes

So deliciously pure and substant

And now I ask myself to leave, to move on

But what of this stirring call

Papatuanuku asks me to come feed of her milky breasts

I choke thinking of moving from this exquisite nutrient from the air aue the air

And what will be the hum of her breath

And what will cradle and smother me like her arms

The whea of the valley the whea of our souls.

– Alison Holden.

THIS PAGE. Mt Aspiring reflected in a tarn on Cascade Saddle.
Colin Monteath/Hedgehog House.
RIGHT. Climbers on the Bonar Glacier. Mt Aspiring's South Face illuminated by the
dawn light. *Geoff Wayatt/Hedgehog House.*

INTRODUCTION

I n the 1950's you could wander up a valley in the Southern Alps and climb a peak and not know how high, how far, or how hard it would be to attain the summit.

Now *not* finding out this information is difficult if not impossible. Not finding out information about mountain routes requires turning a deaf ear to all the helpful advice and maybe not consulting this guide. Instead head to the hills, pick a line or peak that appeals and try climbing it. You may have an epic, but then again you might discover something beyond just climbing.

However if you do choose to read on, this guide will help with access, huts, tracks and route descriptions. A few things have changed in this book, the revised version of Graham Bishop's *The Mount Aspiring Region*. The grades have been adjusted to compare more with the Mount Cook region, which could cause some grief but there are enough technical routes in the area to warrant this change. Route descriptions are now arranged by massif rather than using a hut as a reference point. Other more dramatic and important changes have occurred in the form of rebuilt huts and more bridges. The glaciers are still retreating in the face of rising temperatures and lack of snowfall. These changes are happening quickly so use some of the information in this book carefully; it is a guide not the gospel.

GENERAL INFORMATION

The Mount Aspiring region is special. Mellow grassy valleys lead to backbreaking grinds through steep bush to the prize of wild open snowfields and rugged rocky and icy summits.

The climbing ranges from hands-in-pocket strolls to steep technical classics. This is a user-friendly area, almost as if it was created for mountaineering.

The geographical scope of this updated guide takes in the head of the Dart River Valley to the south, through the central Aspiring region and to the mountains rising from the Wilkin and Young Valleys to the north. This is a broader area than covered by the original Mount Aspiring guidebook.

Road Access

The main road access to the Mount Aspiring region is via the Matukituki Valley from the Central Otago town of Wanaka. The roadhead in the West Matukituki Valley, known as Raspberry Flat, is 53 kilometres from Wanaka.

Wanaka is a rural tourist town situated on the shores of Lake Wanaka. It has the facilities and stores to supply most of your needs. There is a good supermarket and climbing equipment and information is available at Goodsports (03 443-7966) and The Adventure Centre (03 443-9422).

Mount Aspiring National Park

Mount Aspiring National Park was proposed as far back as 1936 by the New Zealand Alpine Club's (NZAC) Otago Section. It wasn't until 1964 that it came into being.

The Department of Conservation (DoC) Wanaka Office (03 443-7660) is located on the left hand side of State Highway 89 when approaching town. There is another DoC office in Makarora (03 443-8365) which serves as a base for the Wilkin/Young area. Other DoC office locations include Queenstown, Glenorchy (for the Dart Valley) and Haast.

Housekeeping

Climbing parties are asked to record their intentions and sign out on completion of their trips at either DoC Wanaka or Makarora. Nocturnal visitors will find the intentions book in a box beside the front entrance of each office. Failure to record intentions or sign out can cause costly and unnecessary searches. Search and rescue is co-ordinated by the Wanaka Search and Rescue team through the Police and National Park staff. Radios are situated in French Ridge, and Colin Todd Huts. During the summer Dart, Top Forks, Young and Siberia Huts have wardens with radios. They can be used to contact the DoC Wanaka Office in an emergency. Search and rescue is a costly and often hazardous exercise—ensure the situation is a genuine emergency before activating a search.

The Wanaka DoC Office keeps a record of route and glacial conditions and posts a mountain forecast daily. Also the local guiding companies can be useful for information regarding mountain conditions. And if you can track down a crusty looking local, they might be able to help. Hut fees can be paid in advance at either DoC office—these fees barely cover the costs of maintaining the huts concerned. Failure to pay hut fees may result in the loss of our alpine huts.

One of the greatest costs is flying out human waste so both the mountains and mountaineers stay healthy. With the advent of climbers 'flying in', a lot more food is taken in than is generally needed. Leaving perishables in the hut may seem like a nice idea, but it turns the hut into a high-altitude compost heap. Take the perishables out and ask yourself is there really any need for another bag of rice or muesli to be left behind.

Guiding Companies

There are three locally based guiding companies: Mountain Recreation (03 443-7330), Mount Aspiring Guides (03 443-9422) and Adventure Consultants (03 443-8711). All offer experienced guides and services that range from basic instruction courses to guided ascents of Mt Aspiring. See the Service Listings section at the rear of this guide for more information.

Geology

The story so far, courtesy of Duncan Ritchie.

The rock in this area is schist, 200 million years old. Which sounds old but it is only a blink of the geological eye.

Greenschist, which is by far the most predominant, comprises two main types of rock: psammatic and pelitic. The psammatic rock is coarser and forms coherent good solid rock. The pelitic rock is fine grained and slate-like, and can be very broken. It is often referred to as choss or weet-bix, and some other unsavoury names.

The greenschist has a volcanic source and some of the mineralogy is altered to chlorite and epidote, giving the green colour. The greenschist is psammatic and forms layers within the greyschist, obvious because of their colour, often tens of metres thick and are usually very solid rock. There is a layer of this rock at Phoebe Creek and a section of this rock there is a crag developed for rock climbing. The climbing is of a very high standard.

Other rock types which exist in the area include rare chert layers (near Colin Todd Hut), marble layers and the spectacular pink piedmontite schist. An example of this rock can be viewed on the side of the Wanaka Library. Thick quartz veins are found within the schist, generally providing good climbing.

Structurally, the schist in this area dips to the west at angles of between thirty–fifty degrees creating slabby west facing ridges and faces, and steep craggy east faces commonly with small overhangs e.g. East Face of Pope's Nose. This is partly due to uplift

9

on the Moonlight Fault and partly to the general structural pattern of the area—large ten kilometre plus scale folds, like pushing a table cloth into ripples.

The significant Moonlight Fault which begins near Queenstown and runs through Lochnagar and past the East Face of Pope's Nose and East Face of Mt Fastness strikes in a nor-nor-east direction and forms the eastern boundary of the highest mountains. It has helped form some of the steep east faces like the East Face of Fastness and Pope's Nose and may be responsible for the Mt Aspiring area being lifted high above the other Otago rock to the east.

Weather

New Zealand is an isolated landmass, surrounded by hundreds of kilometres of lonely ocean. Moisture laden winds, usually from a westerly quarter, blow across the Tasman Sea.

The Southern Alps are the first objects this moisture encounters and they are subjected to the full force of the rainfall. Forecasting the weather in these mountains is notoriously difficult, it can take years to learn the subtleties of wind direction and whether the 'Mares Tails' are the harbingers of bad weather or just swatting flies.

Only general rules of thumb can be used when trying to decipher the weather. Never trust a thumb, it'll end up getting smacked and turning black. Witchcraft and intuition can be more useful when dealing with this fickle beast. Changes in the weather may occur with dramatic and incredible force within the space of a few hours, sometimes with little or no warning.

Although having said all that, one of the rules is: the prevailing west to northwesterly wind precedes the approach of a low pressure area and may be accompanied by very heavy rain, commonly lasting several days. As the low pressure area and its related frontal system pass overhead, the rain will ease to showers and the winds will move back to the southwest, with a temperature drop bringing snow, often as low as the bushline (1000m) even in summer. The period of low temperatures is usually of a short duration and is followed by rising pressures and clearing skies. A good weather forecast with accurate maps is posted at the local DoC office and you can check out the weather when signing in. An easterly weather pattern can be a trap to those in the valley floor who think the thick layer of cloud above is all doom and gloom. The opposite is usually true, for above 1000m there are blue skies and light winds. This is caused by anticyclonic weather, with a temperature inversion causing the blanket of cloud. This type of weather mainly occurs during winter. The Wanaka area can suffer for weeks from this oppressive gloom.

330 millimetres (13 inches) of rain in 26 hours have been recorded at the old homestead of Mount Aspiring Station at the start of the East Branch of the Matukituki where the mean annual rainfall is 2490 millimetres (98 inches). The rainfall at Aspiring Hut is estimated to be about 40 percent higher.

The most settled period is from late December to early March, with February being the best month, remembering these are only general rules. In winter July or August tend to be best although temperatures may be very low. Spring is volatile. One last piece of wisdom regarding the weather. A fine spell sometimes lasts only three days. So walk in on the clearing day, climb the next (the one fine day) and walk out or watch the cloud build and wind rise on the third day.

In winter, spring and early summer there is considerable risk of large scale avalanches in the valley heads and on the steeper snow slopes. River levels during spring and early summer fluctuate considerably on a daily basis in response to the effects of warm northwesterly winds on the thawing winter snows.

Nature of the Climbs

The climbing in the Mount Aspiring region is as varied as the weather. Snow and ice is the main medium to be climbed on but some stunning alpine rock exists in the region.

Ice can be found on south faces from August till Christmas and often outside this time (the South Face of Aspiring can hold good ice at any time of the year). Ice on east faces is more fickle in its formation but can generally be in condition from July to September. Mixed rock and ice can be found on all routes at any time of year.

The rock varies from one mountain to another in its hardness and quality and can vary widely even on the same peak—a ridge that on one side is a desperate shattered pile of horrendous choss can have on the other good solid rock with easy protection.

For many years the reputation of the region was for choss, rubbish and weet-bix, but now with climbers venturing onto steeper faces, more palatable, good clean rock has been found to be more common than previously thought.

Since the first edition of *The Mount Aspiring Region* in 1974 there has been a steady depletion of glacial ice and recession of all the glaciers. Some routes have over time become more difficult or demand a higher level of protection than was once necessary. Some of the standard access routes have likewise become more difficult such as the east side of the Dart Icefall, the Breakaway and the Quarterdeck. There will be seasons when these routes become impassable or require a larger quota of persistence and sneaky rope tricks once the winter snow pack recedes.

Grading

Grading of alpine routes is a contentious issue and will be debated until the mountains are piles of sediment on a future seafloor! To take it too seriously is to waste energy best conserved for loftier things.

The grading system used here has been adapted from the *Mount Cook Guidebook* (Hugh Logan, 1994, NZAC). It aims to give the climber an idea of how relatively hard or easy something is and is the standard grading system for alpine routes. It is widely in use throughout New Zealand.

Take the grade with a grain of salt particularly as some routes have only been climbed once or twice.

The grade reflects the technical difficulty of a route when in condition i.e. an ice route when the ice is formed well or a rock route in summer conditions. 'In condition' itself is a broad term depending on your comfort level, some ice routes can be more fun when thinner or a rock route more interesting with riming. For example the North Buttress of Aspiring is a good mixed route when covered in rime. Isolation is also taken into account when sticking a number on a mountain.

In cases where a climb has a specific rock crux or is predominantly rock, an additional rock grade follows the alpine grade in brackets, for example:

The North Face. Been On A Bender. Grade 5 (18)

Rock grades used in the guide are from the Australasian Ewbank system. This is an open ended system, using whole numbers, currently from 1–34. See the rear of the book for an international grade comparison table.

Waterfall routes are graded with the North American WI system—see the Waterfall Ice section starting on page 117 for more information on this.

As a guide for grading

Grade 1	Easy Scramble. Use of rope generally only for glacier travel.
Grade 2	Steeper trickier sections may need a rope.
Grade 3	Longer steeper sections generally. Use of technical equipment necessary. Ice climbs may require two tools.
Grade 4	Technical climbing. Knowledge of how to place ice and rock gear quickly and efficiently a must. Involves a long day.
Grade 5	Sustained technical climbing. May have vertical sections on ice.
Grade 6	Multiple crux sections. Vertical ice may not have adequate protection. Good mental attitude and solid technique necessary. May require a bivvy on route and be a long way from civilisation.
Grade 7	Grade 7 and beyond is possible but not yet established in the region.

Note: A plus or minus is incorporated into the grade if a particular route is near the top or bottom of a grade.

New routes, updates and corrections

If you've climbed a new route or have comments relating to the omission, clarity, or accuracy of information contained in this guide please do not hesitate to write to:

NZAC Publications, PO Box 786, Christchurch
or e-mail: publications@alpineclub.org.nz

Update information concerning this guidebook, when available, can be obtained from the NZAC website: www.alpineclub.org.nz

HISTORY

Possibly the first mountaineers in the Aspiring region were the Maori people, although their wanderings had a definite goal of real substance other than reaching the summit of a peak. They passed through the area on their way to collect pounamu (greenstone) from the West Coast and used the Haast Pass, Maori Saddle, Harris Saddle and the Greenstone Saddle to travel from east to west. They observed and named avalanche areas, calling them hukahoro. A glacier was hukawai and fresh snow soon to become ice, hukapa.

The mountains were ancestors and landmarks to navigate by. Mount Aspiring is known by the name Tititea, the upright glistening one. There is an unwritten ethic of not standing on the summit of Aspiring out of respect for these ancestors.

Fog and Niger Peaks may be the earliest peaks to have been climbed in the area, when they were ascended by James Park and Alexander McKay during their geological exploration of the Matukituki Valley in early 1881.

But it would have to be Mount Aspiring that is the drawcard for mountaineers. This *'glorious pyramid of ice and snow'* was seen and named by surveyor J T Thomson in 1857. Fifty two years elapsed before it was first climbed by Major Bernard Head, Jack Clarke and Alec Graham on November 23, 1909. Their route, following an abortive probe up the East Matukituki, was up the west face from a camp site on French Ridge. A year earlier Alec Graham had been with Dr Ebenezer Teichelmann and Dennis Nolan when they had explored the northern approaches from the Waiatoto River, but had run out of time with the mountain almost within their grasp.

In November 1929 the fourth ascent was made by a guide called Frank Alack, Jack Aspinall (manager of the Mt Aspiring station) and Lilian Familton. Familton was the first woman to reach the summit of Aspiring. She had a vested interest in the surrounding countryside as she and her brother Ken were part owners of the Mt Aspiring Station.

There is an appealing purity to the sweeping curve of Aspiring's South West Ridge, especially when viewed below your heels. This purity has made it one of the classic ice climbs of the Southern Alps. The first ascent, using step cutting techniques, was made by Harry Stevenson, Doug Dick and David Lewis on December 12, 1936. David Lewis went on to become a renowned ocean-going sailor.

The Otago Section of the New Zealand Alpine Club was formed in 1930 and many peaks were bagged for the first time in the ensuing 10 years: Mt Aeolus, Castor, Alba, Maori, Rob Roy and Avalanche.

There are some mountaineers who have made the Aspiring region their own and this is so with the likes of Paul Powell and Graham Bishop. Powell completed much exploration in the region, claimed several first ascents and wrote some great books about his adventures. Bishop stamped his mark on the area by authoring the original guidebook, studying the Dart Glacier, and making first ascents like the gnarly East

13

Ridge of Rob Roy. His work on the stopbanks around the Aspiring Hut was instrumental in saving the hut from a large slip. If anyone reflects the love and passion for the Aspiring area it is Graham Bishop.

The construction of Aspiring Hut (1944–49) ushered in a golden era and a lot of the mountains radiating off Aspiring were climbed.

Another person who in recent times could take the Aspiring area and trace its valleys and ridges like the creases on the back of his hand is Geoff Wayatt. He moved his fledgling Mountain Recreation business there in the early seventies. Since then Wayatt has made over sixty ascents of Mount Aspiring, which some might say could get a little mundane but then you only have to look at his office and be slightly jealous. Guiding on Aspiring has been made even more accessible with helicopter landings on Bevan Col, and is a growth industry.

Technical mountaineering on steep faces in the Aspiring region has moved slowly. It was thought of as an area where you picked a mountain and started climbing from the valley floor and stopped on a summit, without too much preamble in between. The South Face of Aspiring was where the first action happened, with Pete Moore and Revill Bennett summiting the face in a snowstorm in December 1971. Then Don Bogie and Lindsay Bell climbed the North East Face of Aspiring, sticking their necks out a long way in the depths of winter 1978.

The 1980s were relatively quiet for new routes but Brian Weedon stood out as someone who lusted after virgin ground. He put up the *Shiny Beast* on the South Face of Aspiring with Neil Whiston in December 1981 and *Been On A Bender* on the North Face of Aspiring in March 1981, ushering in not only a couple of good routes but imaginative names as well. Allan Uren and Phil Penney noted that the South

Original Colin Todd Hut, 1987. North West Ridge of Aspiring in the background. *Allan Uren.*

Face of Maori hadn't been climbed and in 1987 made the first ascent of the face, which avoids the horrendously loose East Ridge.

Most of the difficult climbing has been accomplished in winter when the east faces wear icy jackets. The East Face of Pope's Nose was a shady wall that intimidated most—until Nick Cradock came along, near the end of his careering drive as a world class mountaineer, and claimed the first ascent of the face (*F*** the Pope*), over two days in winter 1990, along with Brian Alder, Dave Fearnley and Lionel Clay.

Pope's Nose has some fierce real estate and will be the sight of future struggles. Which is true of the summer possibilities as shown by Dave Vass and Richard Turner's climb of the face in summer—a modern rock route of excellent quality.

Nick Cradock and Brian Alder leading out on the first ascent of the East Face of Pope's Nose, winter 1990.
Lionel Clay/Hedgehog House.

In July 1997 Clinton Beavan, Al Wood and Allan Uren shuffled up the East Branch of the Matukituki and made the first winter ascent of the East Face of Fastness. The climbing of this face in winter was to be the last of the big faces climbed in the Aspiring region in winter. But rather than shutting the door on future fun on big steep scary things—it has shown just how much scope there is for other interesting climbing in the area.

Constructing the original French Ridge Bivouac

From the *New Zealand Alpine Journal*, 1940.

Climbers visiting the Otago mountains will be pleased to know that when next they plan a few nights on the ridge of Mt French they will not be made the sport of our old friend who so often swoops down over Hector Col, nor will there be any argument as to who should carry the tent, for they will now find a very comfortable and roomy little hut perched high and dry at 5,200ft.

The hut stands as a fine example of Club spirit and co-ordinated effort, and none know it better than all those willing helpers who swagged the hut materials and door (generous gift) up two thousand feet of very steep bush-clad hillside and twelve hundred feet of tussock ridge.

We who re-assembled the hut finally on the site can claim little of the credit, as this was a very easy task when compared with the hours of labour expended by Jack and Jerry Aspinall in packing the material to Pearl Flat and by Christmas packing parties.

The idea of this hut first took concrete form at the annual meeting of the Club Committee held last June in Christchurch. Plans and costs were submitted to this meeting, and authority granted to proceed with the work.

The hut was cut out and temporarily erected in Dunedin, then transported to Pearl Flat in time for the Cascade Camp. To remove any doubts as to why the camp was held, I assure members that the hut material was there because of the camp and not *vice versa*.

The rest of the story is well known to most. Glossing over a lot that occurred between Pearl Flat and the hut site, we take the tale up again at Easter 1940, when three from Oamaru—official builders—and a party of about eighteen Dunedin enthusiasts, un-official carpenters, secondary carpenters, stone-wallers, cooks, porters and climbers, assembled at the hut site with all the hut equipment and much impedimenta. The weather was such as we all dream of but seldom realise—calm, sunny days and romantic nights of full moon. The foundation stone was laid on Saturday morning, and the last nail driven on Tuesday night.

The hut is quite easily seen from above and below, and is situated at the final merging of snowgrass and scree. The equipment is most lavish, consisting of cooking utensils, knives, forks, plates for eight people, a two-burner stove, eight sleeping bags and two mattresses, three dozen clothes pegs, coat hangers, mouse-traps, corkscrews and crown top openers, and various other items too numerous to mention.

The interior is lined with 'Tentest' and sheet iron, and, we hope, all points where snow can enter have been blocked with carpet felt. The bunk is built to hold six or seven, and can be folded up by lifting the front portion and sliding it back over the rear portion.

I cannot speak too highly of the excellent state of preservation in which all the material arrived on the ridge. This reflects very creditably on the careful handling by all those who helped transport the material over extremely difficult country, and made the task of erecting the hut much easier than it might otherwise have been.

The hut being finished, on the Wednesday we decided to celebrate, so made an epic ascent of Mt. French with the aid of an assortment of tent-poles and ice axes. After an exceptionally pleasant week we retreated down the valley and through the Gates of Death, pursued by the desultory firing of an approaching nor-wester. *Abridged.*

—H J Stevenson.

USING THIS GUIDE

Rather than using huts or valleys as the main reference points, the climbing routes in this guide have been arranged by massif. For example, some of the massifs are: Aspiring, Avalanche, Rob Roy, Fastness, the Haast Range and Barff.

In some instances this method is impossible to follow. Unfortunately mountains refuse to conform so easily, and climbs are described from the host glacier that flows from their flanks, such as the Bonar, Dart, and Volta Glaciers. Then there is one more minor variation for those routes that are total rebels and they are described from Cascade Saddle, Ruth Flat and Aspiring Hut.

It will be necessary to use the following access routes to plan the best way of reaching the climbing route in question. Where necessary the access routes are cross-referenced with the climbing routes.

➡ Note. The tramping terms *true left* and *true right* have been adopted in this guide and are used even when on a glacier. When you are **facing downstream** (or in the direction of flow on a glacier) *true left* refers the left hand side and *true right*, the right.

Mt Aspiring Hut and West Matukituki Valley.
Colin Monteath/Hedgehog House.

17

Mt Aspiring

Bevan Col

Breakaway

Mt French

Quarterdeck

Mt Avalanche

Mt Joffre

Flightdeck

Mt Bevan

French Ridge

Liverpool Biv.

Pearl Flat

Shovel Flat

Aspiring Hut

MATUKITUKI - MT ASPIRING REGION ACCESS

Having your own vehicle is an advantage but transport 'up the valley'(up the valley is the locals term referring to the land beyond Glendhu Bay) can be arranged through Goodsports (03 443-7966) or Edgewater Adventures (03 443-8422). Transport companies come and go; for up-to-date information contact the Information Centre in Wanaka (03 443-1233).

From Wanaka the road skirts Lake Wanaka and then follows the Lower Matukituki Valley. There is great rock-climbing on the schist bluffs, (which are *roche moutonées* left behind by the last glacial advance) in the lower valley. A comprehensive guide-book, *Wanaka Rock*, is available from the local climbing shops, DoC and the BP petrol station.

The road continues up the valley and is generally easily passable in a two wheel drive vehicle. Be warned, the road has many open fords which can be impassable after heavy rains.

Mount Aspiring Station, the home of John and Sue Aspinall, is the last homestead on the road. Three kilometres beyond the homestead the road comes out onto Cameron Flat at the junction of the East and West branches of the Matukituki River. The road continues up the West Matukituki for eight kilometres passing by a footbridge which provides dry access to the East Matukituki. The road ends at Big Creek on Raspberry Flat and has a parking area with toilets.

Other means of access

The Aspiring region can be reached by cross country trips up numerous valleys including the Dart, Wilkin, Arawata and Shotover. The excellent tramping and backcountry guide; *Moir's Guide North* (available from the NZAC and many major bookstores) can help with these approaches.

West Matukituki Valley Huts

Most of the huts in the West Matukituki Valley are owned by the NZAC and managed in conjunction with DoC.

None of the high huts have stoves or eating and cooking utensils. There are mattresses and radios and solar powered lights in Colin Todd and French Ridge Huts. Hut fees should be paid at DoC in Wanaka or to wardens when in residence.

Cascade Hut (440m)

Cascade Hut was built by the NZAC in 1932 and has the ghosts of climbers past rattling around the roof in a nor-wester. It is situated on the bush edge about two hours from the road end. At present it is kept locked and a booking system operates. Contact the Otago Section of the NZAC: **www.osonzac.org.nz**

LEFT. View of the West Matukituki Valley, French ridge and the Aspiring massif, en route to Cascade Saddle. *Colin Monteath/Hedgehog House. 2000.*

Aspiring Hut (450m)

Built between 1946 and 1949 by the NZAC, Aspiring Hut occupies a beautiful site on the bush edge on the true right bank of Cascade Creek. The hut has accommodation for about 25. Gas cookers are available during the summer months. A hut warden is in residence from November to April. **Time from road end 2.5 hrs.**

Liverpool Bivouac (1065m)

Built in 1953 by the NZAC, but now owned by DoC, the bivvy is a small corrugated iron shelter with shelf type bunks for 8 people. Liverpool Bivvy is situated on the lower slopes of Mt Barff. Access is via signposted track from Pearl Flat. **Time from road end 6-8hrs.**

French Ridge Hut (1480m)

The original bivvy was constructed by the NZAC in 1940 but was destroyed by the accumulation of snow in 1946. It was re-sited and rebuilt in 1949 and lasted till 1973 when a larger hut was built to replace it. The old bivvy remained in use until the early 1980s. The larger hut was replaced with another new hut by the Otago Section of NZAC in 1999. There are warden's quarters and bunks for 17 people. **Time from road end 6-8hrs.**

Colin Todd Hut (1800m)

The original hut was built by the NZAC in 1960, but not before the materials had been airborne eight times and eventually dropped in the wrong place, on the Therma Glacier three hundred metres below the top of Shipowner Ridge. A new hut was built in 1995 and sleeps 12. During the summer months the hut can become very crowded and it is a good idea to inquire as to the availability of a bed at the Wanaka DoC office or at Aspiring Hut.

West Matukituki Valley access routes

A1. Raspberry Flat car park to Aspiring Hut. 2 hours.

This is a pleasant wander up the flats on the true right of the West Matukituki River. A four wheel drive track on the Aspinalls' property (no public vehicle access) reaches all the way to Aspiring Hut. There is a spot about fifteen minutes up the track where the South Face of Rob Roy can be viewed. This view can be a bit like speeding through a small town—blink and you'll miss it, so watch out. The track is gently undulating all the way, apart from a climb over a bluff at Wilson's Camp. This section of track was constructed so a truck could get through with building materials for Aspiring Hut. It is called Gillespie Street after the architect who designed it.

A2. Aspiring Hut to Cascade Saddle and the Dart Glacier. 5–6 hours (to saddle).

A well-travelled and maintained track starts 100m south of Aspiring Hut. Above the bushline the track climbs steeply up a tussock spur marked by orange standards. The route then descends to cross Cascade Creek just above the gut leading to Head's Leap and then sidles round towards Cascade Saddle.

To access the lower Dart Glacier sidle round and across the moraine wall of the Dart Glacier to a flat bench opposite Mt Edward. Beware of avalanches here coming off Plunket Dome in spring and early summer—choose your campsite accordingly!

Also be aware when descending from Cascade Saddle into the Matukituki—spring and early summer avalanches can be encountered and the snowgrass can be treacherous when wet. To ski tour up Cascade Saddle is difficult due to the steep constricted terrain.

A3. Access to the Upper Dart Névé.

Recommended access to the Upper Dart Névé is over Plunket Dome as the icefall is generally too broken to traverse. It could be possible to sneak

Upper Matukituki Valley.
Geoff Wayatt/Mountain Recreation.

up the true right of the icefall after a high snowfall winter. Access is also possible on rock to the west if not threatened by avalanches.

A4. Aspiring Hut to Pearl Flat. 1.5 hours.

Cascade Creek is bridged a few 100m upstream from Aspiring Hut. If the creek is low and Aspiring Hut doesn't need to be visited, (Aspiring Hut has flush toilets, use them) then it is quicker to carry on along the four wheel drive track past Aspiring Hut and cross Cascade Creek by a ford on the track.

The track then carries on up through short grass and intersects the DoC foot track near a patch of bush. In a few minutes the track descends to Rough Creek, which is bridged. Continue through more bush for one hour until Shovel Flat is reached. At the north end of Shovel Flat the track re-enters the bush for a few minutes before emerging onto Pearl Flat.

A5. Route from Shovel Flat to the western side of Rob Roy. 2.5 hours.

At Shovel Flat on the true left side of the river is the beginning of an ill-defined track. It is at the bottom of Shovel Flat about 300m upstream from the beginning of the narrow gorge. It may or may not have ribbons marking the start. A route climbs through bush then into a slip slightly to the north which it follows to the sub-alpine scrub, passing around a few overhangs on the way. A cairn marks the top of the route at the snowgrass and scrub boundary.

Another hour of wandering directly up takes you to a pile of jagged rocks under a high cliff. A number of bivvys are found here, the best holding 3-4 people. Another bivvy can be found higher up approximately 200m south of the col at 1750m en-route to the West Face.

A6. Pearl Flat to Liverpool Bivouac. 2 hours.

The track to Liverpool Bivouac starts on the north side of Liverpool Stream. Cross using the bridge if necessary. The track climbs steeply up through the bush at a sign near the junction of Liverpool Stream and the Matukituki River. Above the bushline the track leads to the right on steep exposed shingle and tussock. This is a dangerous spot if wet or snow covered and was the scene of a fatal fall. Once easy tussock slopes are reached bear left to reach a knoll overlooking the bivvy. Avoid sidling across to the hut below this knoll when the hut is first sighted. You'd end up in tiger country with steep bluffs and may never be seen again.

A7. Liverpool Bivouac to Arawata Saddle. 4-6 hours.

This is a difficult packing route, involving steep snow or rock slopes with danger from avalanche and rockfall from Liverpool. From the hut follow up the stream for a few minutes before crossing the low ridge to the south and descending a cairned track to cross the first stream off Mt Barff. Sidle left to the small knob ahead, then bear right to cross the next creek. Climb out on to the moraine wall and follow along its crest to the steeper slopes directly below the saddle. On starting up these move initially to the left for 100m or so and then gradually move out to the right, to gain the northern end of the saddle.

There may be no snow below the saddle late in the summer, in which case some short and steep rock steps will be encountered. A more detailed route description can be found in *Moir's Guide North*.

Routes from Pearl Flat to the Bonar Glacier

From Pearl Flat the Bonar Glacier may be reached by way of French Ridge, French Ridge Hut and the Breakaway or Quarterdeck routes. An alternative is by means of the Bevan Col route from the head of the valley. French Ridge is the most straightforward route but French Ridge Hut is a long way from Mt Aspiring. The Quarterdeck can be broken, crevassed, and requires travel very close to the lip of Gloomy Gorge.

The Breakaway was quite dangerous during the 1980s, but has recently become more attractive access to the Bonar Glacier. The Bevan Col route is technically more demanding and it is a longer day getting to Colin Todd Hut but once there you are poised, closer to Mt Aspiring. The Bevan Col route is dangerous in the winter and early spring due to avalanche hazard in the lower gut.

➠ It should be noted that the Bonar is subject to fog and white-out conditions and a compass is mandatory for travel in such murk.

Mt Aspiring

Mt French

Breakaway

BONAR GLACIER

South Face
of Mt Joffre

French Ridge Hut

French Ridge and Mt Aspiring. From left to right - NW Ridge, West Face, SW Ridge,
South Face, Coxcomb Ridge. Lines indicate approximate routes to The Breakaway and
Quarterdeck. Note: The Breakaway route is subject to significant summer avalanching.
Colin Monteath/Hedgehog House.
⏩ See also photo on page 79.

Upper French Ridge, looking up to the Quarterdeck, Mt French up in the clouds. *Duncan Ritchie.*

A8. Pearl Flat to French Ridge Hut. 3.5 hours.

The track to French Ridge Hut climbs from the West Matukituki on the true left of the river at Pearl Flat. Either ford the river here or if the river is in flood continue upstream to a signposted turn-off to a swingbridge. This option will take about 20 minutes more. The track is very steep but has user friendly tree roots to haul body and pack up on. The track emerges on gentler tussock slopes which are then followed up for another 400m. The spectacular ravine to the right as you climb is known as Gloomy Gorge.

The hut is situated on a flattish spot just below the normal snowline. The upper part of the route is very exposed to the weather.

A9. Pearl Flat To French Ridge via Scott's Bivvy. 4 hours.

This is an alternative route to French Ridge Hut, not often used. There is no track after leaving Scott's Bivvy. Follow the track into the head of the valley and from Scott's Bivvy climb directly away from the river in scrub and tussock slopes, crossing a dry rocky creek bed high up, before continuing up another 100m on slopes of short grass which lead up to a small steep spur between two slabby faces. Follow this spur out to the old hut site on French Ridge, a few metres above the French Ridge Hut.

A10. French Ridge Hut to the Bonar Glacier via The Breakaway. 2.5 hours.

The Bonar Glacier is accessed from French Ridge by either the Breakaway or the Quarterdeck, both these routes may require complex route finding through crevasses in summer conditions.

The Bevan Col route to the Bonar Glacier from the head of the West Matukituki Valley. French Ridge in the right foreground. *D L Homer, NZ Geological Survey. Feb 1979.*

To access the Breakaway ascend the cairned route from French Ridge Hut to an elevation of 1800m, traverse due north from here maintaining your elevation and gaining height as you near the Bonar. Be warned, the Breakaway breaks up rapidly (not surprisingly) as the winter snow pack melts and is always exposed to rockfall and avalanche danger from the slopes of Mt French. The Breakaway is a better winter than summer route. From the top of the Breakaway to Colin Todd Hut takes about 1.5 hours.

A11. French Ridge Hut to the Bonar Glacier via The Quarterdeck. 2.5 hours.

This is the best route to take onto the Bonar unless the Breakaway is in good winter-like condition. The Quarterdeck is the shoulder gained by following a snow ramp from the top of French Ridge to the true right of Gloomy Gorge. It is generally straightforward early in the summer but opens up radically through the season and crossing crevasses and the bergschrund may prove problematic in late summer.

Currently (2001) the Quarterdeck has been able to be reached even when very broken, by passing the initial crevasses on the true right under the Mt French rock cliffs then traversing right to gain slabs and climb the ridge on the edge of Gloomy Gorge. The Quarterdeck is exposed to slab avalanches during winter.

A12. The Bevan Col Route from Pearl Flat to Colin Todd Hut. 8 hours.

The track continues up the valley on the true right from the top end of Pearl Flat. It crosses a major avalanche chute coming off Mt Barff before emerging from a patch of ribbonwood on to the open scrubby area in the head of the valley. About 10 minutes later bluffs force a crossing to the true left of the river. A walkwire has been installed here to allow safe crossing of the river.

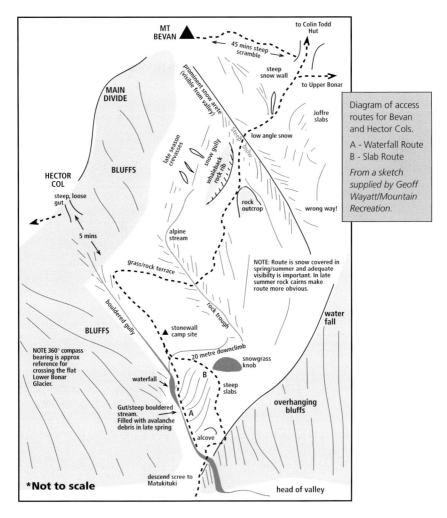

MT BEVAN

45 mins steep scramble

to Colin Todd Hut

steep snow wall

to Upper Bonar

MAIN DIVIDE

prominent snow arete (visible from valley)

Joffre slabs

low angle snow

Diagram of access routes for Bevan and Hector Cols.

A - Waterfall Route
B - Slab Route

From a sketch supplied by Geoff Wayatt/Mountain Recreation.

HECTOR COL

steep, loose gut

5 mins

BLUFFS

late season crevasses

snow gully

whaleback rock rib

steep snow

rock outcrop

wrong way!

alpine stream

grass/rock terrace

NOTE: Route is snow covered in spring/summer and adequate visibilty is important. In late summer rock cairns make route more obvious.

bouldered gully

rock trough

water fall

BLUFFS

stonewall camp site

NOTE 360° compass bearing is approx reference for crossing the flat Lower Bonar Glacier.

20 metre downclimb

snowgrass knob

waterfall

B

steep slabs

overhanging bluffs

Gut/steep bouldered stream. Filled with avalanche debris in late spring

A

alcove

descend scree to Matukituki

head of valley

*Not to scale

Oate's Rock Bivvy (800m) is slightly downstream of this crossing. It is more salubrious than Scott's Bivvy but may be challenging to get to if the side stream flowing into the Matukituki is in flood. The bivvy is visible from where the West Matukituki track breaks out of the bush. On the true left of the Matukituki and downstream of a sidestream flowing into the river are three large boulders. The uphill one is cairned, as is the bivvy. Cross the river on the walk-wire and head up the sidestream on the true left for 100m to cairns, which mark a small normally dry watercourse. Follow this back down valley until a track heads left. This leads to a clearing where the track peters out. Climb up 30m to the bivvy. At the moment it would sleep three people securely in a nor-wester and with some judicious shifting of rocks, three more could be 'inserted'.

Inclement conditions on the Waterfall/ Gut route to Bevan and Hector Cols. *Geoff Wayatt/ Mountain Recreation.*

To reach Scott's Bivvy cross the Matukituki and follow cairns on the true left of the river. After following the river for 200m a faint track leads away from the river and after crossing two streams, Scott's Bivvy (790m) can be found. It is marked with a cairn on top. This bivvy has a low roof and a claustrophobic air about it. It is generally damp and has a resident stream running through it when it rains.

An ill-defined track, though well cairned, continues up valley from the true left side of the bivvy. After crossing a stream issuing from near the Breakaway, open tussock slopes lead up towards the waterfall pouring from a narrow gut at the head of the valley. Moraine slopes, then a deer trail lead around and into the gut, where the stream is crossed immediately above the waterfall. Continue on the true left up easy slabs and tussock until a broad ledge is reached about 20m above the stream. From this ledge there are two alternatives. The best route is to continue up the slabs keeping at a fairly constant height of 10-15m above the stream, along a series of discontinuous ledges.

Most of the route is on sound rock and although a few moves may be found difficult with a heavy pack, a rope is not normally required. The alternative route follows a prominent deer trail which leads back to the ridge overlooking the head of the Matukituki, climbing high before returning to the slabs well above the stream. The rock on this variation is technically no easier than on the recommended route but is much more exposed, especially as a packing route. The gut is subject to avalanche hazard, especially in the lower part during winter and spring.

The gut opens out into an upper basin, up through which the route continues until about 70m below Hector Col, where easy slabs lead up and eastwards around to a broad ledge that extends across the South Face of Bevan. Follow this ledge, climbing gently, until a rock rib leading directly up the slope towards Bevan and marked by a large cairn is reached. Climb either this rib or the easy snow alongside until a sharp snow arête, very obvious from down valley, is reached. Cross the arête and continue on an ascending sidle across easy snow into Bevan Col at 1851m.

After crossing the col and dropping about 30m towards the Bonar Glacier the Colin Todd Hut can be seen across the glacier at about the same altitude as the col on a bearing of 360 degrees magnetic. It is sited at the top of a prominent snow tongue leading from the glacier on to the crest of Shipowner Ridge. From the col to the hut takes about one hour. From the head of the valley to the hut takes about five hours and most parties take at least 10 hours from Aspiring Hut.

A13. Colin Todd Hut to Aspiring Hut. 7 hours.

On the reverse trip care should be taken not to commence sidling towards the basin below Hector Col before the broad ledge running across the South Face of Bevan is reached.

A14. Matukituki Saddle and Hector Col.

Hector Col is now not normally attempted, as an easier descent can be made from Matukituki Saddle. To get to the Matukituki Saddle and Hector Col follow the Bevan Col route (A12) to the top of the gut at the head of the valley. The Matukituki Saddle is reached by heading up easy tussock slopes aiming for a point about one kilometre south-west along the Main Divide from Hector Col. Hector Col is right at the head of the upper basin. The ridge is steep, exposed scrambling.

Hector Col was reached and crossed by Dr James Hector, J W Sullivan and an assistant named Rayer, on February 11, 1863. They threw their packs down the northern side, and went on to record a remarkable achievement in reaching within eight miles of the West Coast before starting the long journey back to Otago. These pioneers were plagued by wet weather and only had two days' food, which they eked out for two weeks. By the time they regained their food dump in the Matukituki their menu had degenerated to toi-toi root soup and boiled sheepskin.

In more recent times—the 1990s, a party took a wrong turn when descending Bevan Col in the mist. Before they realised their mistake they had descended down Hector Col and into the wild Waipara Valley. Imagine their dismay at finding their detour had taken them into an isolated West Coast valley rather than the friendly Matukituki. Thinking it would be easier to forge on out to the West Coast they bush-bashed down valley. Two days later, feeling a lot worse for wear (they too had run out of food, but didn't know about toi-toi soup or boiled sheepskin) they arrived at the Haast–Jackson Bay road. They then hitched a ride to the pub at Haast and salvation.

A15. Rob Roy Stream to Rob Roy/Homestead Col.

Rob Roy Stream drains the Rob Roy Glacier and joins the West Matukituki 30 minutes walk from the road end. A spectacular view of the South Face and East Ridge of Rob Roy can be had from this junction.

A swing bridge crosses the West Matukituki and a good track leads through the bush to above the bushline, 2–3 hrs.

To reach the col which lies at the head of this valley continue up the true left of the stream until a large slip is reached. Climb up this until it nearly peters out, then head out left onto terraces and traverse towards the glacier without gaining too much height. There is a large flat terrace overlooking the lower Rob Roy Glacier. Cross this and descend onto the rubbly glacier. From here take the spur that leads onto the snowfield aiming for the low point of the ridge between Rob Roy and Homestead Peaks. Time from the bush line to the col, 5–6 hrs.

A16. Rob Roy/Homestead Col to Avalanche Glacier and beyond.

From the col ascend the East Ridge of Rob Roy for about 50m and gain a broad ledge that traverses north and can be seen from the lower Matukituki Valley. This ledge provides spectacular year-round access to the Avalanche Glacier. From the Avalanche Glacier it is possible to access the Bonar Glacier region by traversing the Avalanche Glacier, crossing the Rob Roy/Avalanche ridge at it its low point and continuing via the Maud Francis Glacier and the Flight Deck to the Bonar. This is particularly interesting as an alternative route out of the Bonar region at the end of a trip.

East Matukituki Valley

The quiet beauty of the East Matukituki so impressed Duncan Macpherson, one of the early run-holders, that in 1898 he cut a track as far as Junction Flat, where he built a hut in anticipation of the tourist trade. The madding crowd failed to materialise however, and the East Branch has in fact had considerably less development than the West Matukituki. Consequently it has retained a special charm of its own, including some magnificent river and bush scenery. There are no huts in the East Matukituki.

A17. Cameron Flat to Rock of Ages Bivvy. 3.5 hours.

Ford the West Matukituki and continue up the vehicle track towards the old Mt Aspiring Station homestead. The ford is not suitable for cars and may be unsuitable for people after heavy rain, in which case a swing bridge about 3km up the West Matukituki may be used. From the ford to the old homestead is about 20 minutes and the start of the Glacier Burn which drains the Avalanche Glacier is a further half-hour up the flat.

The Glacier Burn is like a child's secret place, and is somewhere to go and contemplate on a sunny summer's day. Opportunities for climbing are few but it does afford access to the East Ridge of Avalanche by following up the large tributary coming in on the north side. Cross this tributary below a gut a few 100m above the junction, then follow up grassy slopes below the bush and scrub until tussock slopes lead directly to Duncan's Knob.

The track up the East Matukituki carries on up the true right of the valley after crossing the Glacier Burn on a swingbridge at the bush edge. Junction Flat at the confluence of the Kitchener Stream is reached after 3 hours.

29

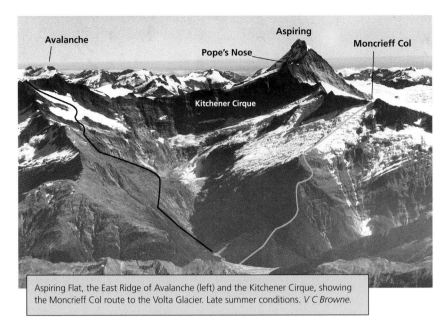

Aspiring Flat, the East Ridge of Avalanche (left) and the Kitchener Cirque, showing the Moncrieff Col route to the Volta Glacier. Late summer conditions. *V C Browne.*

From Junction Flat a well marked track leads up the Kitchener. It then emerges on the extensive and swampy Aspiring Flats. Follow around the swampy area by keeping close under the hill until the forest closes in to the river again. It is possible when the flow is low to wade a braid onto the gravel flat and walk up the valley. The Rainbow Valley joins the Kitchener from the true left and a short distance upstream of the junction, on the true right of the Kitchener is the aptly named Rock of Ages Bivvy (520m). This massive rock is set in the bush about 20m above the river. The well-worn track up to the bivvy is marked by a cairn. The bivvy provides reasonable shelter for 6 to 8 people. There is room for 10 to 20 but shelter would be indifferent, especially during a north-westerly storm.

Aspiring Flat

The views from Aspiring Flat are stupendous and the river issues from the Kitchener Cirque by way of an impressive 370m high waterfall. The cirque was first breached by Jock Sim, Scott Gilkinson, Russell Fraser and Eric Strang, in 1933. They climbed the steep bush and scrub south of the waterfall before descending into the upper basin and climbing out to the Main Divide at Parachute Pass. Unfortunately the ill-aimed and high-velocity arrival of their air-dropped supplies forced an end to their trip.

Aspiring Flat is the launch pad for climbing Mts Aeroplane, Avalanche, Fastness, Moncrieff and Sisyphus.

A18. Rock of Ages to Hood Glacier.

From Rock of Ages Bivvy follow the track on the true left of the Kitchener Stream for 10 minutes until opposite Spurling Creek which drains from the East Ridge of Avalanche. Head up Spurling Creek until the bottom of a broad spur which tapers to a point at the bushline on the true left of the creek.

Continue up the spur until underneath a line of bluffs then sidle west through the scrub for half an hour. Alpine scrub is the last defence left to the Hood Glacier and may need a large dose of patience to be negotiated. Watch out for conquistadors!

Easy travel through tussock along broad benches leads westward to a prominent knob overlooking Turnbull Thomson Falls, which drain the Kitchener Cirque.

From this knob a broad easy ridge leads up to scree level. Screes are traversed westward down to a narrow notch in the rock rib falling to the north from the east ridge. Beyond the notch several hundred metres of slabs give access to the lower eastern tongue of the Hood Glacier, which is traversed horizontally for about one kilometre until a broken icefield leads to the upper névé. From the head of the névé a short but steep rock climb leads to the summit ridge between the east and the middle peaks.

The rock notch can also be reached from the col between Duncan's Knob and the East Ridge (approached either from Aspiring Flat or Glacier Burn - page 29) by sidling the first knob of the ridge on the north side on an exposed deer trail, and then traversing, on a gradual descent, the snowgrass ledges and snow on the north side of the ridge.

A19. Rock of Ages to Moncrieff Col. 10–12 hours.

Access to the Volta Névé. The Moncrieff Col route was pioneered by Paul Powell, Brian Wilkins, Ian Bagley, Colin Todd and Arthur Tyers, between October and December, 1951.

The route is not marked but follows the leading ridge separating the Kitchener and Rainbow Valleys. This ridge is gained by a subsidiary bush-clad spur on the south (Kitchener) side, almost opposite the Rock of Ages Bivvy. The ridge above the bushline is narrow and exposed to the weather, with few campsites and little water.

There is a small but good bivvy rock on the ridge above the bushline (at about 1300m) which sleeps 3 people. It stays dry during a nor-wester. At about 1400m the ridge runs out into bluffs which are turned on the north-east side, at first on steep snowgrass, but eventually on easy rock ledges which allow a return to the broad snow ridge above. Easy but heavily crevassed slopes, especially after Christmas, lead up towards the col, with the angle steepening considerably in the last 100m or so, where a large schrund usually develops.

A20. Junction Flat to Ruth Flat

Walkwires have negated the need to brave the difficult fords across the Kitchener Stream and the Matukituki. There is a well marked track which starts on the true right of Hester Pinney Creek. It climbs steeply up through the bush. Above the bush

Access

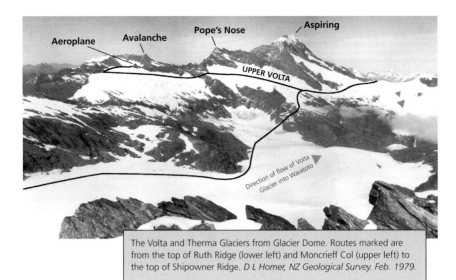

Aeroplane Avalanche Pope's Nose Aspiring

UPPER VOLTA

Direction of flow of Volta
Glacier into Waiatoto

The Volta and Therma Glaciers from Glacier Dome. Routes marked are from the top of Ruth Ridge (lower left) and Moncrieff Col (upper left) to the top of Shipowner Ridge. *D L Homer, NZ Geological Survey. Feb. 1979.*

the route is marked by orange standards which mark the way up valley. One to two hundred metres more in height are gained until a scrubby ledge is reached. Ruth Flat is visible from here. A sharp descent leads back into the bush, through which the track gradually descends towards Ruth Flat.

A21. Ruth Flat to the Wilkin Valley

There is a good route description for this route in *Moirs Guide North.*

A22. Ruth Flat to the Volta Névé via Ruth Ridge. 5–6 hours.

The first party to reach the Volta from the east were Howard Boddy, Bill Wilson, Sid Studholme, Geoff Pryor and Jim Shanks. They ran into trouble, when on the descent Studholme slipped and injured his spine. The race against time for help and the subsequent battle to bring a stretcher down the Bledisloe Gorge rate high in the successful chapters of New Zealand mountain rescue before the advent of helicopters.

From the junction with the East Matukituki continue up Ruth Stream until a suitable route leading onto the crest of the ridge to the north is found, on the east side of the avalanche fan leading from the higher part of the ridge. The ridge steepens to a narrow snow arête with a final pitch of steep, loose rock.

➠ Warning: Neither the Moncrieff Col nor Ruth Ridge routes offer an all-weather escape route from the Volta Névé.

A23. Volta Névé to Colin Todd Hut from the top of Ruth Ridge. 12–15 hours.

Follow down the lateral trough of the Upper Volta to skirt the West Ridge of Fastness, descending the icefall on the true left/east side. It may be necessary to climb over the end of the West Ridge if the icefall is badly broken. Head across the the main Volta Plateau towards a snow route leading up to the Upper Volta Shelf near the toe of the North East Ridge of Aspiring, where some big crevasses can be expected. Skirt the toe of the ridge on a flattish area, wasting no time crossing the big avalanche tracks from the ice cliffs above. From here further crevassed slopes lead up and around to the upper basin of the Therma Glacier. A final climb of about 150m leads up to the snow saddle between the top of Shipowner Ridge and Rolling Pin, with an easy descent down to Colin Todd Hut, 250 metres below.

This was the route of the first Volta-Therma traverse, by Paul Powell, Colin Marshall, John Sage and Earle Riddiford in December 1945.

A24. From Moncrieff Col. 7–8 hours.

From the col follow easy slopes around the head of the névé to reach the rock step dividing the glacier close to where it joins the Main Divide near Pope's Nose. Although steep, this rock step is not difficult in good conditions, even with heavy packs, and gives access to the heavily crevassed shelf of the Upper Volta. Pick a route down this shelf, parallel but not too close to the North East Ridge of Aspiring, which has a tendency to shed ice and rocks. At the toe of the ridge the route joins the route from Ruth Ridge.

This variation was first traversed by Graham Bishop, Roger Barrowclough, and Henry Stoddart in December 1961.

LOWER MATUKITUKI VALLEY CLIMBS

The mountains in the lower valley can sometimes peek out from behind the rain shadow of the greater alps and provide good scrambling when a mountain fix is desired. The lower valley climbs, apart from the winter waterfall routes, are mostly grade 1–2 requiring little more than an ice axe and crampons. Beware of loose rock.

Craigroyston (2211m)

1.1 The North West Ridge. Grade 1

Pick a route up through the bluffs between Raspberry and Big Creeks, to gain the easy leading ridge. 200 to 300 metres below the summit a steep gut is crossed to give access to a better ridge on the south west side, which is then followed to the summit. The final 50m or so are on relatively exposed slabs. The climb to the summit takes about six hours from Raspberry Flat.
Paul Powell, Geoff Baylis & Len Kitson. Dec 1953.

1.2 The South Face. Grade 1

Start up the tussock and bracken slopes directly behind Raspberry Hut. After about one hour the ridge becomes well defined and eventually leads to a col (1750m) on the Shotover-Matukituki divide. From this col follow a deer trail south for several hundred metres, until the south ridge is crossed and a prominent snowfield on the South Face is reached. The snowfield is then climbed to the summit. This route would take about six to seven hours from Raspberry Flat.
Peter Child, Don Morrison & Chris Matthews. Feb 1969.

1.3 The North East Ridge. Grade 3+

The North East Ridge is reached from the col at the head of Raspberry Creek and consists of a steep climb on shattered rock, with some delicate and unprotected moves, as only this type of climbing can deliver, necessary near the top.
Bill Duffy & Charlie Tanner. March 1975.

Fog Peak (2240m)

1.4 The East Ridge. Grade 2

Steep tussock slopes on the south side of Niger Stream lead out to the ridge between Niger and Fog Peaks. Fog Peak may be reached, either by traversing the rock ridge to the summit, or by cutting out on to the snowfield on the South Face. This is a long climb from the road and would probably take about eight hours to the summit.

1.5 The North Ridge. Grade 1

From Glenfinnan Peak the straightforward rock of the North Ridge leads to the summit ridge some 200m north-east of the summit.

Craigroyston

1.1

Shark's Tooth

1.11

Fog

1.6

1.5

Glenfinnan

View down the West Matukituki Valley from near Wilson's Camp. Early Winter. *D G Bishop. July 1973.*

1.6 The West Ridge. Grade 1+

The West Ridge is reached by crossing the North Ridge between Glenfinnan and Fog Peaks and traversing on suitable ledges across the steep North Face of Fog Peak until the West Ridge provides a straightforward route to the summit. To be climbed comfortably, this route would probably require a camp near Glenfinnan Peak.

Paul Powell & Geoff Baylis, 1963.

Glenfinnan Peak (1890m)

1.7 Via Niger Stream

Glenfinnan Peak is a fine viewpoint overlooking the confluence of the two branches of the Matukituki. It is easily reached in four to five hours from the road by climbing the tussock slopes on the north-west side of Niger Stream.

Homestead Peak (2020m)

Named in recognition of the hospitality of the Aspinall Family of Mt Aspiring Station. Homestead Peak was first climbed by Paul Powell, Owen Wye and Geoff Harrow in December 1952. They climbed the South East Ridge, partly as an exercise in keeping warm, after a stormy night had put paid to their attempt on the unclimbed East Ridge of Rob Roy.

Nine years later circumstances were similar when Peter Strang, John McKinnon, Jim Milne and Graham Bishop, also with eyes on the still-virgin ridge of Rob Roy, briefly escaped from a saturated tent to snatch a new traverse of Homestead Peak by the North West and South West Ridges. In 1968 Brian Cleugh and Jack Coker after admirable persistence finally climbed the long sawtoothed South West Ridge leading to the South Peak.

1.8 From the East Matukituki. Grade 1

Cross the West Matukituki at Cameron Flat to start up the hill immediately behind the old homestead of Mount Aspiring Station, on the south side of Homestead Creek. The South East Ridge is gained above the head of the creek and is a straightforward rock climb the summit. From Cameron Flat to the summit would require from seven to eight hours.

1.9 From Rob Roy Stream. Grade 2

From Rob Roy Stream use access route A15 to access the gentle snowfields in the head of Rob Roy Stream. These give easy access to the North West and South West Ridges, which are both very straightforward rock climbs on rather loose rock. Each ridge takes about one hour from the head of the snowfield.

Niger Peak (2018m)

1.10 Grade 1

Niger Peak is an easy scramble from the road, either by the South East Ridge from just north of Leaping Burn or by the tussock slopes south of Niger Stream. The climb would take about four to five hours from the road to the summit.

Shark's Tooth (2096m)

The spectacular spire of Shark's Tooth was first climbed by Bob Craigie, Phil Cook, Roland Rodda and Scott Gilkison on December 19, 1939.

1.11 The South West Ridge. Grade 1+

Climb to the col on the Shotover-Matukituki divide. An easy tussock and rock ridge, with snow on its south side, leads north east from the col to the final rock pyramid, which is normally climbed by the moderately steep, rather loose slabs of the West Face or the rocks of the South Ridge. Five or six hours are required from Raspberry Flat to the summit.

Black Peak (2289m)

Black Peak is a spectacular mountain in the lower valley with easy access through farmland (please seek permission for this privilege from C Ewing at Cattle Flat Station, phone (03 443-7152) or R Ewing at Matukituki Station phone (03 443-7241).

1.12 Grade 2

There are two main ridges both of which can be seen from Wanaka, the Eastern Spur and the North Ridge. The Eastern Spur is accessed through Cattle Flat Station and is an interesting climb through bluffs and along an exposed ridge. The other route is through Matukituki Station and goes up the true right of Phoebe Creek and under a line of bluffs on a sheep trail then up the ridge.

➠ During winter Black Peak is the site of some steep multi-pitch ice climbing. See the section on waterfall ice, starting on page 117.

CASCADE

Climbs from Aspiring Hut

Mt Ansted (2388m)

Ansted was first climbed by Frank Wright and J R Simpson, from the Dart Valley, on February 21, 1914.

2.1 Via the Cascade Saddle track. Grade 1+

From the top of the Cascade Saddle track, which is marked by a tripod pylon, head south along the ridge towards the low peak of Tyndall, until a suitable line across the Isobel Glacier is reached. Alternatively cross the upper basin of Cascade Creek to reach the easy angled North Ridge. The top fifty metres of rather loose rock are interesting climbing—brush up on the art of climbing choss.

Ansted is a long climb from Aspiring Hut, especially as it is commonly combined with an ascent of Tyndall. The climb to the top of the saddle takes about 4 hours, with a further 3 to 4 hours to reach the top of Mt Ansted.

Glengyle (2283m)

Glengyle is an impressive sight from Aspiring Hut, although it is in fact little more than a bump on the South Ridge of Rob Roy. The crags and towers of Glengyle are sometimes mistakenly called the Cathedral Peaks—however, that name was originally applied to all peaks between Bevan and Glengyle on the northeast side of the West Matukituki.

2.3 The South Ridge. Grade 2

Climb to the ridge by way of a clearing through the bush, across the river and slightly downstream from Wilson's Camp. From the crest of the ridge cross into a basin on the west side of the South Ridge of Rob Roy and traverse across this into a second basin to reach the foot of a mixed snow and rock ridge leading to the summit. The climb requires about 10 hours from Cascade Hut to the summit and a bivvy high on the slopes opposite Wilson's Camp would be desirable. *Ernie Smith, Brian Hill, Bob Fullerton, Les Buddicom, Don Divers, George Edwards, and Russell Edwards, Dec 1934.*

2.4 The West Face. Grade 2

There appears to be no problem in forcing a route up through steep bush into the snow tussock basins below the peak, from where there are a variety of interesting looking rock routes to the summit.

A direct ascent was made from Aspiring Hut in seven hours by Jim Millson, Feb 1976.

2.4a West Face. Following Dave. Grade 3

Access from terminal moraine under Rob Roy.
Dave Fearnley, Geoff Wayatt & followers, Jan 1978.

Governors' Ridge

Plunket Dome

Islington

View up the West Matukituki from near Wilson's Camp. Early winter. *D G Bishop. July 1973.*

Islington (2425m)

2.5 The East Ridge. Grade 2

There appears to be no record of a complete ascent from Shovel Flat although the upper part of the ridge was climbed on January 16, 1970, by Brian Chalmers, Jill West, Judy Knewstubb, Rod McKenzie and Don Murray, who gained the ridge by traversing across the Christopher Johnson Glacier from route 3.2.

Tyndall (2496m)

Tyndall was first climbed by Frank Wright and J R Simpson on February 21, 1914, from the Dart Valley. Mention was made that it had been 'partially ascended' previously, and indeed in 1922 Professor James Park claimed that Alexander McKay, John Buchanan and himself had climbed it in 1881, along with Mt Edward, Mt Ansted, and 'all the high peaks to the south' [of Hector Col].

McKay's account on the other hand, written a few months after their expedition, makes it clear that they only went as high as 'Red Rock' on Tyndall, and indicates that Park's claims to this and the other ascents were probably embellished with the passage of time.

2.6 Via Shotover Saddle. Grade 1+

Start up easy tussock slopes on the down valley side of Tyndall Stream. When approaching Shotover Saddle bear west below the patch of red rock. Traverse through a series of easy snow basins on the north side of the East Ridge into the cirque below the low peak. Steep snow slopes lead out, on to the North Ridge a few hundred metres north of the low peak and an easy slope leads on to the high peak beyond. This is a long climb and would probably take about nine hours from Cascade Hut to the summit.

2.7 Via the Cascade Saddle Route. Grade 1+

From the top of the Cascade Saddle (A2), Tyndall is a very easy climb by the North Ridge, taking about six hours from Aspiring Hut to the summit.

GOVERNORS' RIDGE

Access to Plunket Dome, Islington and Liverpool

Governors' Ridge is the ridge connecting Plunket Dome, Islington and Liverpool and is the edge of the upper Dart Névé. A fantastic alpine wander can be had by travelling up Cascade Saddle along Governors' Ridge and down one of the ridges above Rough Creek.

3.1 Via the Cascade Saddle track. Grade 1+

From the top of the track follow around and through a basin to Cascade Saddle. North of the saddle Governors' Ridge, an easy, broad, but crevassed snow ridge leads over Plunket Dome and Islington to Liverpool. From Aspiring Hut to Liverpool requires about 7 hours.

Governors' Ridge was first climbed by Frank Wright, J R Simpson, Jack Clarke, Colin Ferrier & Bernard Head, Feb 1914.

3.2 Via the ridge north of Rough Creek. Grade 2

From Aspiring Hut cross Cascade Creek (bridged) and strike up through the bush from the top of the flats opposite the hut, to meet Rough Creek at the foot of the hill slope. Cross Rough Creek on avalanche ice to gain the scrubby ridge to the north. The ridge joins Governors' Ridge between Plunket Dome and Islington. The main obstacle is usually a large schrund a short distance below Governors' Ridge.

The first ascent party took five and a half hours to reach Governors' Ridge from a bivvy well above the bushline. It seems likely that this time could be improved considerably in good conditions and a time of six hours from Aspiring Hut to the ridge seems reasonable.

Roland Rodda, Rod Sinclair, Leo Quinn & Ralph Glasson, Dec 1939.

3.3 Via the ridge south of Rough Creek. Grade 2

From Rough Creek (Route 3.2) climb through the bush and scrub of the ridge immediately south of the creek. Traverse left (south) across scree about 50m above the scrub line into a gully. Cross the creek in the gully and work up through the snowgrass bluffs to the south to reach a ridge with a clear gully on either side. Climb straight up the ridge until it peters out level with the snout of a small glacier descending from Plunket Dome. An easy traverse leads across to the glacier, the south side of which is then followed up to Governors' Ridge, about 350m above Cascade Saddle.

This route would probably take about five hours to Governors' Ridge. It was investigated in 1954 as a possible alternative route to the Dart, and remnants of a cut track may be found below the bushline.

THE DART GLACIER

Mt Edward (2620m)

The attractive peak of Edward can be seen from the Raspberry Flat car park in all its glory, over the top of Cascade Saddle. Like a lot of the peaks in this guide that aren't named Aspiring; Mt Edward doesn't see many ascents. The first ascent was made in 1914 by Bernard Head, Jack Clarke and Colin Ferrier, who climbed from the head of the Whitbourn. The first ascent from the Dart was by Russell Gordon, George Edwards and Doug Knowles, on March 7, 1935.

Maoriri

Maori

Aerial photograph of the Dart Glacier.
➠ See photo overleaf for more detail.
Colin Monteath/Hedgehog House, Jan. 2001.

4.1 Via the Marshall Glacier. Grade 2

Cross the Dart Glacier below the icefall to the scree slopes south of the East Ridge. These give access to the Marshall Glacier which is followed up to the base of a prominent rock face on the south side of the East Ridge about 200m below the peak. From this point the ridge is followed, with two chimneys and a short snow ridge before the summit. Alternatively the snow of the South Ridge can be reached by continuing to the top of the Marshall Glacier. The climb would take six to seven hours from Cascade Saddle.

4.2 The East Ridge. Grade 2+

Unfortunately no details of the route are available. The ridge can be gained by climbing the avalanche gully just south of the icefall and traversing a broad ledge (subject to avalanche early in the season) to reach the foot of the East Ridge immediately above the icefall. The lower section of the ridge appears to be the best rock and the most interesting climbing.
Stafford Morse & Russell Fisher.

Liverpool (2482m)

4.3 From the Dart Glacier. Grade 2

This route gives access to the upper basin of the Dart Glacier, where easy crevassed slopes lead up to the peak. The once easy slopes immediately east of the icefall are now generally impassable due to glacial recession. The route to the west of the icefall ascends an avalanche gully until level with a broad ledge which is reached by traversing across steep shingle. This route is threatened by avalanche in early summer. The icefall has been descended on skis in winter during the early 1990s but that may have been an exception. From Cascade Saddle Route 3.1 is a much more direct approach to Liverpool.

Maiti-iti (2460m)

Maiti-iti was first climbed by Lindsay Bruce, Alex Gourlay, and Les and Doug Brough from the Snow-White Glacier in January, 1958. The first ascent from the Dart was by Laurie Kennedy and Bruce Robertson, who traversed from Maori in February, 1966.

4.4 The East Ridge. Grade 2

From the summit of Maori descend the shattered rock of the West Face to the col on the Main Divide. The East Ridge of Maiti-iti is a climb of about 100 metres, consisting of a lower section of loose rock and a more difficult and exposed upper section, before a short snow ridge leads to the summit, about l.5 hours from Maori. The col between Maori and Maiti-iti could probably be reached from the Dart Névé.

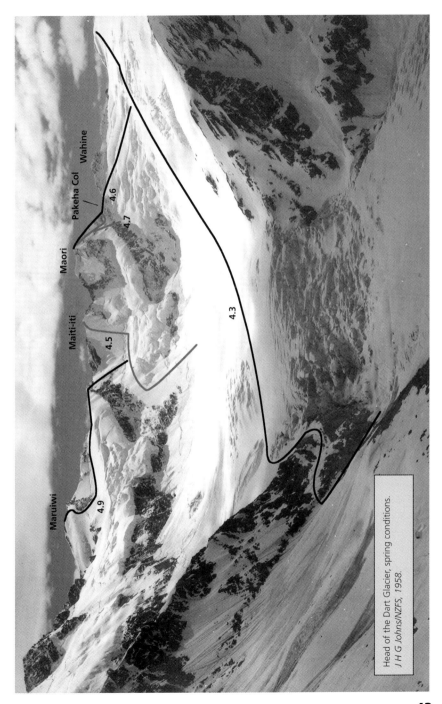

Maruiwi

4.9

Maiti-iti

4.5

Maori

Pakeha Col

Wahine

4.6

4.7

4.3

Head of the Dart Glacier, spring conditions.
J H G Johns/NZFS, 1958.

4.5 The South Face. Grade 2+

The steep snow face of Maiti-iti is reached by climbing straightforward snow slopes beneath the ice-cliffs of the Park Glacier.
Barry Scott & Rob Petit, Dec 1974.

Maori (2535m)

First climbed on March 5, 1935, by Russell and Gordon Edwards, Ernie Smith, and Doug Knowles, Maori repulsed further advances for 25 years, until Les and Doug Brough, Lindsay Bruce, and Alex Gourlay finally succeeded from the Snow-White Glacier after a series of attempts totalling 55 days spread over seven years. The route of the original ascent from the Dart was not repeated until 1966.

4.6 The East Ridge. Grade 3

From Cascade Saddle follow route 3.1 before veering left under the South Face of Wahine to reach Pakeha Col. The route on Maori zig-zags up a series of rotten rock ledges on the Dart Face to regain the ridge above the main gendarme. Above this the rock improves somewhat but is still poor, with some delicate towers just below the summit. The climb would take about five hours from Cascade Saddle and one and a half hours from Pakeha Col.
Russell & Gordon Edwards, Ernie Smith & Doug Knowles, March 1935.

4.7 The South Face. Grade 3

Follow route 3.1 towards Pakeha Col and the East Ridge then drop down to underneath the face. The route parallels the East Ridge through a rock band on mixed ground, and up steep snow slopes to the summit. This is a good mixed route and of better quality than the East Ridge.
Allan Uren & Phil Penney, April 1987. First winter ascent: John Marcussen, James Broadbent, Don French and Nick Groves, Sept 1999.

Maoriri (2595m)

Maoriri was first climbed in December 1937, by George Lockwood, Arch Wiren, and Jock Sim by traversing below the ridge from Edward, but there is no record of a direct ascent from the Dart.

4.8 The South Ridge. Grade 2+

From Edward (route 4.1) a traverse along or below the ridge to Maoriri appears straightforward.

Maruiwi (2460m)

Maruiwi was formerly known as Moriori. The first ascent was by Jim Dawson, Bob Craigie, Phil Cook, and Scott Gilkison on January 7, 1939, from the Snow-White Glacier.

4.9 Via the Park Glacier. Grade 2+

It appears possible to reach the extreme northern end of the Park Glacier by a

Detail of Maori South Face routes.
Winter. *John Marcussen, 2000.*

steep snow face with an upper rock band, at the south-west end of the shelf of the hanging glacier beneath Maiti-iti and Maori. From the Park Glacier the summit could he reached by easy snow routes on either the North East or South Ridges. The snow face was climbed from the Dart Névé by Phil Penney and Simon Harris.

Wahine (2480m)

Formerly known as Ferguson, Wahine was first climbed by Gordon Edwards, Ernie Smith and Doug Knowles on March 12, 1933.

4.10 The West Ridge. Grade 1+

From Pakeha Col (see route 3.1) the West Ridge of Wahine is a short, easy rock climb, taking three to four hours from Cascade Saddle.

4.11 The East Ridge. Grade 1+

Access Liverpool by route 3.1 and traverse the straightforward rock and snow of the Main Divide to Wahine, one hour from Liverpool.

Islington (2425m)

4.12 The North East Face. Grade 2

Follow the route towards Arawata Saddle (A7). After climbing about half the steep section below the saddle access is obtained to a snow shelf leading out to the south-east, which provides a straightforward route to the summit, with two pitches of steep, loose rock to the summit ridge. About five hours out from the hut. With glacial recession this route may be difficult or dangerous from ice and rockfall.

J Strang & party, 1978.

Liverpool (2482m)

4.13 The North Ridge. Grade 3

The North Ridge rises abruptly from Arawata Saddle in two large steps. The lower one appears to be a relatively broad buttress which might best be climbed on the west side. The second however appears to involve a narrow and exposed section of ridge above the second step the angle of the ridge eases and the re-mainder of the climb appears relatively straightforward on the snow slopes or rock slabs west of the ridge crest before a short rock pitch at the top

Dave Brown & Mike Hutchins, Feb 1966. No details of the climb were recorded.

4.14 West Face. Grade 2

From Arawata move south through ledge systems before gaining steep gullies and loose rock below the summit ridge. Climbed from a bivvy below Arawata Saddle. 7 hours return.

Geoff Wayatt & party, Jan 1979.

Climbers in the Upper Dart Névé, heading towards
Mts Maori (left) and Wahine (middle).
Nick Groves, Winter 2000.

MOUNT BARFF (2245m)

Maybe the person who named Barff was sick of mountains when they christened it. From Aspiring Hut Barff is one of the prettiest peaks in the park and is a joy to climb. Being of small stature and on the Main Divide it is one of the first peaks to be cloaked in West Coast clag.

It was first climbed, solo, by Gordon Speden on Christmas Day, 1929. What a great Christmas present that would have made.

From Liverpool Bivouac

4.15 The South West Ridge. Grade 2

The South West ridge is a straightforward mixed climb leading from Arawata Saddle to the lower of the twin summit towers. The prominent step on the ridge above Arawata Saddle (sometimes called Bow Peak) may be traversed, or turned on the Arawata side. The easiest route on the higher (eastern) of the twin summit cones is on the north-western side.

Time to the summit is about five to six hours.

4.16 The South Face. Grade 2

This broad crevassed snow face is reached by traversing towards Arawata Saddle for about half an hour, until suitable access to the snowfield is found. An easy snow climb then leads to the rocky summit cones (see route 4.15). This is probably the quickest route on Barff and would take three to four hours in good conditions. Large schrunds which have developed in recent years near the top of the face may be difficult to cross.

First climbed on December 27, 1939, by two parties: consisting of Jack Aitken, Roy Stroud, Jock Toomey, and Bert Ouelch, with Eric Miller, Dot English, Angus Black, and Len Chant.

4.17 The South East Ridge. Grade 2

The South East Ridge may be gained more or less directly above the hut. A few gendarmes low on the ridge provide interesting but rather time-consuming climbing; however they may be avoided by following the route towards Arawata Saddle (A7) for a few minutes and striking up towards the ridge, on the west side of the prominent rock bands north-west of the hut. Above the gendarmes an easy snow ridge leads to the higher of the twin summits; this is best climbed from the north-west side. Just below the twin summits a large schrund has formed which requires some delicate climbing with an indecent amount of exposure down a gully to the West Matukituki to spice things up.

The time from the hut to the summit is about five to six hours.

Fred Gallas, Lyall Blackie, Sam Parker and Dot Green, Dec 1939.

4.16

4.17

South Rib

Bow Peak

Arawata Saddle

Liverpool Biv.

Mt Barff, South Face. Bow Peak is indicated at left, as are directions of travel for Arawata Saddle and Liverpool Bivouac. ◢ Note: The South Rib route is not described in the text. *Geoff Wayatt/Mountain Recreation.*

4.18 The North Ridge. Grade 3+

The North Ridge is a much more demanding climb than any of the other recognised routes on the mountain. To get to the North Ridge use access routes A12 and A14.

From Matukituki Saddle the ridge consists of easy rock and snow as far as its junction with the ridge separating the Arawata and Waipara watersheds. Three prominent buttresses follow. The first is climbed by a steep rock couloir to gain a snow ridge above, from where an easier mixed section leads to the second buttress. This is the crux of the climb as it overhangs slightly at the bottom and although the rock is sound, there are few holds. Brown and Hutchins climbed it direct but a break in the west side may offer an easier route.

The upper part of the buttress consists of a smooth vertical face at the top of a sharp snow arête, and was turned on a narrow and exposed crack on the eastern side of the ridge. The third buttress is climbed by a crooked chimney well round on the west side. Above this steep snow leads to the summit towers, of which the easternmost is the highest and is climbed by easy rock on its north-west side.

The first ascent was made in heavily iced conditions and took about nine hours from Matukituki Saddle to the summit.

Dave Brown & Mike Hutchins from a bivvy on Matukituki Saddle. Oct 1966.

Rob Roy (East Ridge)
2644m

Homestead Peak
2020m

Mt Avalanche
2602m

Mt Aspiring (South Face)
3033m

Pope's Nose (East Face)
2700m

Some of the Aspiring region's classic peaks viewed from the entrance to the East Matukituki Valley. *Allan Uren.*

MOUNT ASPIRING/TITITEA (3033M)

Mount Aspiring is usually reached from Pearl Flat. From the flat the following access routes can be used to gain the climbing routes: A8, A9, A10, A11 and A12. French Ridge Hut (A8 & 9) can be used as a base to climb the South West Ridge and South Face. A8 is the preferred route.

Bevan Col (A12) accesses Colin Todd Hut, which can be used as a base for the North Buttress, North West Ridge, South West Ridge and the Haast Range.

➠ Note. In winter or early spring it is recommended to use the French Ridge access routes to get to the Bonar Glacier. After the spring avalanche cycle, or when the Quarterdeck becomes impassable, use the Bevan Col route.

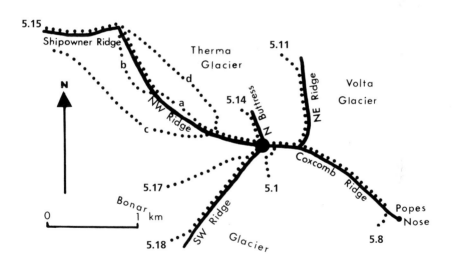

LEFT: The western and southern aspects of Mt Aspiring reflected in a tarn on Cascade Saddle. *Colin Monteath/Hedgehog House.*

Mt Aspiring

The South Face of Mt Aspiring. Winter.
Duncan Ritchie.

The South Face

The first ascent of the South Face was made by Pete Moore and Revill Bennett on Christmas Eve, 1971. The climb commenced as a reconnaissance in deteriorating weather at 2pm and was concluded, 12 hours later, in a snowstorm. A bivouac was attempted on the face but in the absence of adequate bivvy gear it was soon abandoned and the climb continued. Subsequent attempts to dig in were also abandoned due to cold and lack of food and the descent was eventually commenced at 2am, French Ridge Hut being regained at 9am.

The second ascent was made by Bill Denz and Limbo Thompson in early May 1972. They started up the face at 1pm bivvying as darkness fell, about 50 metres below the upper part of the Coxcomb Ridge before completing the climb and returning to French Ridge the next day.

A direct finish to the route (see photo at left) was made by Moore and Bennett in August, 1973. A variation (at left) including the lower rock band was climbed by Ken Hyslop and Neil Whiston in January 1976.

5.1 Original - Moore & Bennett. Grade 4+

This route on the South Face involves a climb of 530m from the foot of the face. It generally parallels the South West Ridge up a series of small snow ramps and intervening rock steps, until below the very steep rock face directly beneath the summit. Here there is a prominent snow arête which is crossed and a rising traverse is followed until the exit gullies are reached. There are a number of these all of a similar grade.

Pete Moore & Revill Bennett, Dec 71.

5.2 Denz & Thompson. Grade 4+

Denz and Thompson turned the bottom rock band by way of the ice cliffs above the schrund at the western end of the rock band. The upper part of the route sidles beneath the summit rock face until better angled ice slopes lead out on to the snow arête of the upper Coxcomb, about 50m below the summit.

Bill Denz & Limbo Thompson, May 72.

5.3 Quite Direct. Grade 5

A direct finish variation which avoids any sidling and tops out on the summit. When the prominent snow arête below the summit rock band is reached go straight up and climb a narrow five metre ice pillar sandwiched between a slab on the left and an overhanging wall on the right. Then there are 3-4 pitches up a gully which ends on the summit.

Allan Uren, Oct 1993.

5.3a Santa Claws. Grade 4+

An ice climb on the leftmost part of the South Face. Start as for route 5.1 but continue directly up to the schist headwall above (rather than following the right tending ramps of 5.1 & 5.2). At the headwall follow a ramp that climbs

5.11

5.8

5.10a

5.9

East Face of Pope's Nose 8.2

Pope's Nose (foreground) and the Coxcomb Ridge of Aspiring (5.8). North East Ridge (5.11) at right. *D L Homer, March 1976.*

Close up aerial shot of Coxcomb Ridge (centre) and South Face (left). *Chris Rudge/Hedgehog House.*

rightward. At the top of this a rock and ice chimney (crux) breaks through the headwall to join the Summit Ridge. Cross over this ridge into the gully at the top of the South West Ridge and continue up easy ground to the summit. Completed in 52 hours return from Christchurch.
Alex Palman & Daniel Druce, July 1995.

5.4 Mixed Aspirations. Grade 5+

This is a fine line tackling the bottom rock band at its proudest point. The rock band is the most difficult climbing and is generally of a mixed nature. At about three quarters height the route joins the other routes and finishes up the Moore direct finish. 12 pitches.
Pete O'Connor & Bruce Hasler, summer 1997.

5.5 The Whiston & Hyslop Line. Grade 5+

Starts out right through the bottom rock band onto the ice field mid-height, then angles back left diagonal towards the summit and the normal exit gullies. About 10 pitches were climbed after the rock band.
Neil Whiston & Ken Hyslop, Jan 1976.

5.5a Leo Hugo. Grade 5

Starts just left of The Shiny Beast, linking together two ice ramps.
Antoine Cayrol & Francois Bernard, Dec 2002.

5.6 The Shiny Beast. Grade 5

A steep nine pitch ice route. There were about four pitches through the bottom rock band and then a couple of easier pitches that were climbed simultaneously. Then a mixed pitch to join the Coxcomb about halfway along the ridge. Required a bivvy just below the 'Coxcomb'. The Beast being the ice; it was green and glistening but good to climb.
Brian Weedon, Neal Whiston, Dec 1981.

5.7 The Chocolate Fish Route. Grade 4

This slash on the right side of the face was used as a variant start to the Coxcomb. The route is nice straight up ice climbing and a wonder-filled start to the Coxcomb. Some of the route approaches vertical but bridging eases the strain. Five full fifty-metre pitches.
Allen Uren & Clinton Beavan, summer 1997.

5.8 The Coxcomb Ridge. Grade 4

The first ascent of this long impressive ridge was made by Roy Beedham and Stuart Holmes on January 11, 1953. Two years previously, however, what very nearly turned out to be a successful ascent was made by D W Peacock, N O'Neill and M Pemberton, more or less by accident. After reaching a point estimated to be about 70 metres below the summit at 7pm they elected to retreat, eventually bivvying on the ridge at about 2835m, before returning to French Ridge the next day, minus success and the seats of their trousers. A few days later, having reached the summit by a more ortho-dox route, they were ruefully able to identify the point they had reached.

North East Face of Mt Aspiring, Pope's Nose at extreme left.
Geoff Wayatt/Mountain Recreation.

5.10a

5.10

5.9

8.2

UPPER VOLTA

Moncrieff Col to Colin
Todd Hut route

The ridge is reached from the head of the Bonar at a snow col just west of Pope's Nose. A lower set of gendarmes are rather rotten, but above these the quality of the rock improves. Most parties have preferred to keep to the northern side of the ridge as much as possible to avoid verglas. Near the top of the lower section of gendarmes is a prominent overhang, which has been turned on either side. The overhang is followed by a long snow arête, towards the top of which the Coxcomb is joined by the North East Ridge. Above this is a further series of gendarmes separated by snow or ice arêtes and including a three metre drop which is usually jumped, or can be rappelled if necessary, before a final short snow arête leads to the summit.

Times for the route vary greatly. The ridge has been climbed in 5 hours; however, most competent parties in ropes of two could expect to take about 8–9 hours.

Roy Beedham & Stuart Holmes, Jan 1953.

5.9 Dave & Richard's Route. Grade 5 (20)

A quality modern rock route up an elegant buttress. The route takes a line up the buttress to the left of the North East Face following perfect crack systems. It starts on a small slab at the toe of the buttress. The problem is getting into this route. Dave and Richard rappelled down off the Coxcomb from the Bonar, a somewhat committing prospect. If snow conditions allow there is a snow ramp down off Pope's Nose but this breaks up quickly.

Dave Vass and Richard Turner, summer 1998.

5.10 The North East Face. Grade 6

The North East Face was climbed by Lindsay Bell and Don Bogie in August, 1978. Bivvys were necessary at the bottom and top of the climb. Bell and Bogie reported that due to the poor nature of the rock and the risk of stonefall, the climb would only be practicable when iced up. The route starts out to the left of the obvious ice streaks running down the middle of the face and then, when roofs are encountered traverses into the main streak, which usually has clean rock to the right of it.

Lindsay Bell & Don Bogie, August 1978.

5.10a James Langley Wags Work. Grade 5+ (18/19)

An excellent line that follows nine pitches of very good, weathered rock, before deteriorating as it nears the North East Ridge. Climbed in 12 x 60m pitches. To descend, the first ascent party partly descended the North East Ridge before making four 50–60m abseils to the glacier.

Russell Braddock & Dave Vass, summer 2003.

5.11 The North East Ridge (Surgeon Spur). Grade 3

The North East Ridge separates the Volta from the Therma Glacier. It was first climbed independently by two parties, Lindsay Bruce, Ian Bagley, Brian Wilkins, and Reg Scott, from Otago; and Dick Tornquist, Ivan Pickens, Jack Rattenbury, and J D

Mt Aspiring, North East Face (right), North Buttress (centre) and North West Ridge on left. *Geoff Wayatt/Mountain Recreation.*

Rockell, from Auckland, on January 4, 1955. The Otago party spent four nights out, two in a snow cave where the ridge meets the Coxcomb. To add to their discomfort they received shocks during an electrical storm.

The whole epic makes absorbing reading and may have deterred subsequent attempts. However the third party on the climb found the route to be both practicable and enjoyable. It should be noted that the ridge merges with the upper part of the Coxcomb (route 5.8) and that the most difficult pitches occur on the latter.

> Access from the top of Shipowner Ridge is by traversing the basin of the upper Therma and then up easy crevassed slopes to where the ridge is gained, either by the highest continuous snow tongue on to the ridge or by slabby pitches above a large rock tower, two to three hours from the hut. The ridge is exposed and generally of shattered rock; however, a long sidle on the eastern (Volta) side, about 15 metres below the ridge crest, allows many of the steeper pitches of the lower part of the ridge to be avoided. A more difficult section occurs higher up, before 200 metres of steep snow lead on to the Coxcomb Ridge. The remaining part of the Coxcomb appears to require at least as much time as the North East Ridge. The climb, including a descent by the North West Ridge (route 5.15), has been done in 12 hours.

5.12 The North Face. Grade 3+

> The North Face, described as an enjoyable climb on good rock, follows a rock rib up the centre of the face before a section of mixed climbing leads into the Coxcomb Ridge, about 600 metres below the summit. Access to the start of the climb via the Therma Glacier is rapid and easy (see route 5.11) This route and *Been On A Bender* are best attempted when riming on the Coxcomb is light, otherwise bombing, resembling the Blitzkrieg could be encountered.
> *Ken Hyslop & Don Bogie, Jan 1978.*

5.13 The North Face. Been On A Bender. Grade 5 (18)

> The climb has a brilliantly sunny aspect. It offers best conditions in late summer although access into the Therma Glacier could be a problem (see route 5.11). It follows the less prominent rib up the face right of the Bogie/Hislop route. Eight pitches on the steep part of the face through a series of small overhangs on good rock. A further six rock pitches to the Coxcomb. Fourteen pitches in all. Fourteen hours return from Colin Todd Hut.
> *Mark Edgar & Brian Weedon, March 1981.*

5.14 The North Buttress. Grade 3

> The North Buttress is a strangely neglected route, offering as it does a direct and exacting rock climb on the sunny face of the mountain, with amazing views of the ocean as you're climbing.
>
> From the crest of Shipowner Ridge descend into the upper basin of the Therma Glacier and cross easy crevassed slopes to the foot of the buttress. Easy slabs soon steepen to a 60 degree prominent light grey band, the top of which is

Mt Aspiring

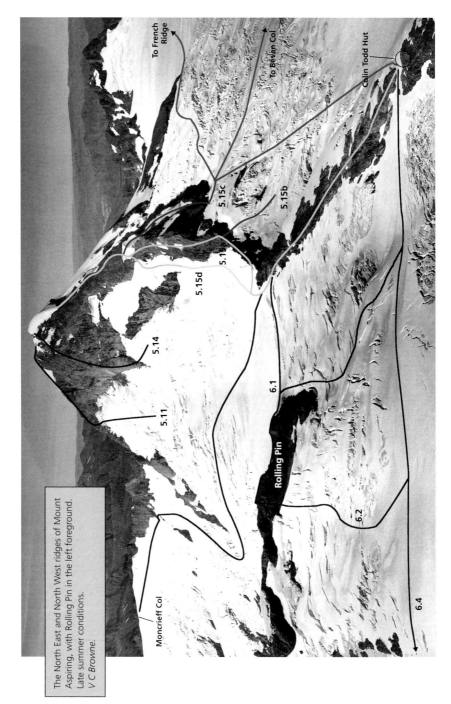

The North East and North West ridges of Mount Aspiring, with Rolling Pin in the left foreground. Late summer conditions.
V C Browne.

about a third of the way up the climb. Cross the slabs going from right to left and go across a ledge which is very exposed over the North Face. Then follow the crest of the buttress. A series of gullies on the North Face should be on your left. Near the top of the buttress broken rock just to the east of the ridge crest is followed by a short pitch of snow before the final rock step, which is turned by shallow gullies on the east. A short snow or ice slope then leads directly to the summit. The rock grade is about 13 and if it gets any harder than that then you are possibly off route. When the buttress is iced up with riming the mixed climbing is good. Beware of falling ice.

The first ascent began as a reconnaissance, but even with a three-man rope the climb was completed from the foot of the buttress in the remarkable time of 3 1/2 hours.

Peter Robinson, Dick Irvin & Roland Rodda, Jan 1956.

5.15 The North West Ridge. Grade 2+

The North West Ridge was first climbed by Samuel Turner, Harold Hodgkinson, Jack Murrell and George Robertson on March 11, 1913, during the second ascent of the mountain. After climbing French Ridge and the Quarterdeck, they then travelled down the Bonar to reach the ridge near its junction with Shipowner Ridge.

The exposure and difficulties of the climb were subsequently greatly exaggerated by Turner, who concluded that 'the first climb and probably the last of Mount Aspiring's east precipices was finished'. Turner was geographically disoriented; his 'east precipices' were actually the northern slopes of the buttress, and their route, far from being avoided, has become instead the most popular on the mountain. Nevertheless, the achievement of this party, torn as it was by acrimonious bickering and with only one experienced mountaineer in its ranks, should not be underrated. Their climb involved more than 60 hours without sleep, including a bleak benightment in a storm above the buttress before continuing the descent in rain and wind the next day.

Following are the variations of the North West Ridge route (5.15a–d).

5.15a Grade 2+

From the hut Shipowner Ridge is followed to 70m below its junction with the North West Ridge, from where easy snow immediately below the rock on the north side leads around to the lower, level, gendarme-studded section of the North West Ridge. All the gendarmes may be turned or traversed easily. As the ridge starts to rise towards the big rock step of the buttress a prominent sloping slab leads out and around on to the Therma Face. After a short, steep pitch a series of ledges and intervening rock steps may be traversed on an ascending diagonal line until the ridge is regained at the level section above the buttress (2400m). Alternatively a route may be made directly up the Therma Face of the buttress and then along the crest of the ridge. Above the buttress a broad easy angled ridge of snow or slabby rock leads to the ice cap and the short, but narrow and exposed summit ridge. This route can be accessed from the Bonar

Mt Aspiring

Mt Aspiring. From left, North Buttress, North West Ridge, West Face and South West Ridge. Fastness (left) and Pope's Nose (right). Late summer conditions.
V C Browne.

Glacier by traversing north 400m from the start of route 5.15c.

5.15b Grade 2+

The lower section of the North West Ridge below the buttress may be avoided by descending to the Bonar from the hut and regaining the ridge at the foot of the buttress. It is doubtful if this variation is any faster than route 5.15a, and it is certainly less interesting.

5.15c The Ramp. Grade 2+

The lower part of the North West Ridge and the buttress may be avoided by descending to the Bonar from the hut and following up easy crevassed slopes to where a steep snow or ice ramp (45–55°) on the south face of the buttress leads up to the level section on the ridge above. Rock showing through on the bergschrund of the ramp may cause considerable difficulties in late summer (grade 13) and windslab avalanche conditions may be encountered from wind loading from the west at any time of the year.

➠ **This route has been the scene of several fatalities. The factors of late afternoon soft snow and a steepening slope require extra caution.**

5.15d Grade 2+

In early summer rapid access to the ridge above the buttress may sometimes be gained by descending from the top of Shipowner Ridge into the Therma Basin and crossing easy snow below the North Face of the buttress to a point where an all snow route leads back to the ridge. This route, on the sunny face, is soon cut by schrunds as the season progresses. This is also a good descent route early season. A rappel can be made from the flat spot at 2470m.

Times for the North West Ridge vary greatly; a rapid return climb time would be 8 hours. The average is 11–12 hours and slow parties have been observed doing overtime up to 18 hours!

5.16 West Couloir. Grade 3

This steep seven pitch couloir provides interesting and rapid access to the North West Shoulder in winter and early summer conditions.

5.16a Forgotten Couloir.

A pleasant, direct line up a 55–65 degree ice couloir topping out on the North West Ridge. In best condition from early summer to January. Approximately eight pitches.

5.17 The West Face. Grade 3

The West Face, route of the first ascent of Aspiring in 1909, was not repeated until 1965, when Jill Tremain and Ian Jowett made the second ascent.

Cross the schrund at the head of the access slopes from the Bonar Glacier and follow up the shallow gully in the centre of the face. A steep rock band cuts across the top of the face and this may be turned by climbing out, either on steep snow slopes to the North West Ridge, or by the couloir at the top of the

South West Ridge (see photo page 64).
Major Bernard Head, Jack Clarke & Alex Graham, Nov 1909.

5.18 The South West Ridge. Grade 3+

This is one of *the* classic climbs of the Southern Alps. The ridge is gained from the Bonar, normally by its western flank at any convenient point below the rock band. About 150m below the summit, the ridge runs out into a steep open couloir, in which ice or even rock is sometimes encountered, before the ice cap and summit ridge are reached.

There are about three 55–60 degree pitches from the bottom of the couloir to where the ridge joins the North West Ridge. These pitches could be regarded as the crux and certainly they have the most exposure, especially combined with the drop down the West Face.

Harry Stevenson, Doug Dick and David Lewis, Dec 1936.

Mt Aspiring's West Face (centre) and South West Ridge (right) during winter.
Duncan Ritchie.

THE HAAST RANGE

The Haast range of mountains is a wild extension of Mount Aspiring running out west towards the sea and becoming more isolated the further from Colin Todd Hut you get. The peaks are described in order starting nearest Aspiring. Stargazer, Skyscraper, Moonraker and Mainroyal are romantic names commemorating the sails of the tall ships and given to the peaks of the Haast Range by Gerhard Mueller in 1885.

Rolling Pin (2249m)

The intriguing name of this mountain, so incongruous in comparison with the nautical names of the other Haast Range peaks, is apparently derived from its resemblance to the culinary instrument when seen from the east. It was first climbed by Allan Evans and Geoff Milne on January 3, 1948.

6.1 The Skyline Traverse. Grade 2

This is a classic traverse taking in mind-expanding views of the Tasman Sea and if reversed, Mt Aspiring. Continue to the top of Shipowner Ridge from Colin Todd Hut and climb the snow and rock arête on to the south end of the summit ridge. The long level ridge is predominantly snow and is very exposed on the Therma Glacier side. Return to the hut via the Iso Glacier. The round trip takes about five hours.

6.2 The West Face. Grade 2

Traverse across the Iso Glacier at about the same height as the hut until underneath the summit, which is reached by easy snow and rock. From the hut to the summit takes about two hours.

6.2a West Face rock routes

Situated on the West Face of Rolling Pin beneath the 35m abseil descent from the main summit, as seen from below, not the abseil at the end of the ridge. There are five routes, ranging from grades 15 to 22, all on natural gear, all single pitches, on clean rock. (They were cairned at the time of their first ascents).
• 2 cracks to the left of the obvious crack/corner.
• The crack/corner itself.
• 2 routes to the right, one of which is a crack the other a broken corner starting underneath an overlap.
Crag best approached from the hut, along the Iso Glacier (the one footing the West Face of Rolling Pin), well worth the walk.
David Hiddleston & Malaysian Alpine Club members, March 1996.

Mainroyal (2266m)

6.3 The North Ridge. Grade 1

Traverse north across the Iso and Dipso Glaciers at about the same level as the hut, until the col between Skyscraper and Mainroyal is reached. A few minutes easy climbing up the rocky ridge leads to the summit, about 2.5 hours from the Colin Todd Hut.

Paul Powell, Leo Faigan, Jack Ede & Gerry Wall, Dec 1948.

Skyscraper (2347m)

6.4 The West Face. Grade 3

From the hut traverse the Iso and Dipso Glaciers at about the same level as the Colin Todd Hut, until the north end of the Skyscraper massif is reached. The route is up a poorly defined buttress on the face, about 200m west of the Skyscraper-Mainroyal Col, slightly east of a short snow tongue. The buttress leads to the summit ridge a short distance south of the peak, which is then reached along easy rock and snow.

The face takes two to three hours and is a sustained rock climb. From the hut to the summit requires about six hours.

Ash Cunningham & Graham McCallum, Jan 1951.

6.5 The East Face. Grade 2+

Follow route 6.9 to the summit ridge of Stargazer and then traverse south to the high col between the two peaks. A steep and rotten, but not difficult rock wall leads to the summit, about six hours out from Colin Todd Hut.

Stargazer (2352m)

Stargazer is the highest of the Haast Range peaks. Until December 17, 1935, when it was climbed by Harry Stevenson, Doug Dick, Stewart Ombler, Scott Gilkison, and Jim Dawson the peak reigned as the elusive virgin of the Otago mountains.

6.6 The East Face. Grade 2+

Climb to the top of Shipowner Ridge and cross the snow saddle leading to the Therma Névé. Traverse on moderately steep snow beneath the rocky eastern faces of Rolling Pin, Mainroyal and Skyscraper to reach the heavily crevassed slopes leading up to the ridge near the centre of the Skyscraper-Stargazer massif. The schrunds under this face may prove difficult, as they appear to have become more pronounced in recent years. The ridge is gained a few metres south of the summit and easy snow leads to the top.

The face may also be reached by crossing the Skyscraper-Mainroyal Col from the west (see route 6.4). A schrund on the east side of the col is sometimes awkward. In good snow conditions the climb should take about six hours from the hut to the summit.

Harry Stevenson, Doug Dick, Stewart Ombler, Scott Gilkison and Jim Dawson, Dec 1935.

6.7 The West Ridge. Grade 3

From Colin Todd Hut cross the Iso and Dipso Glaciers at about the same height

as the hut and follow a steep snow lead up to a level section on the West Ridge, about 300 metres below the summit. The steep rock ridge is then followed, with the more difficult moves occurring on its lower sections. Near the top, the ridge peters out and it may be necessary to move out on to the face to the south to gain the summit ridge, six to seven hours out from the hut.
Ash Cunningham and Graham McCallum, Jan 1951.

Spike (2126m)

The first ascent of Spike was made by Peter Brook, Colin Todd and Kemp Fowler on January 11, 1949.

6.8 The South West Face. Grade 2+

Follow route 6.9 as far as the bench below Spike. The peak is climbed by a snow face on the south west side, followed by 80m of unpleasantly loose rock.

Moonraker (2054m)

The name is more inspiring than the peak, which was first climbed by Peter Brook, Colin Todd and Kemp Fowler on January 11, 1949.

6.9 The North West Ridge. Grade 2+

Traverse the Iso and Dipso Glaciers to the west ridge of Stargazer, which is crossed immediately below two prominent rock steps. The North Face of this ridge is descended by a series of snow gullies and the ridge then followed down about 400m on slopes of snow tussock, until a narrow shelf of snow tussock leads around into the cirque below the North West Face of Stargazer. As the ledge is followed north it becomes broad and sloping and an unpleasant slabby gut has to be crossed before the cirque is reached. From the cirque a snow spur leads out to a broad, gently sloping bench that runs below Spike and continues to the North West ridge of Moonraker. The North West Ridge consists of a short snow climb and 20m of easy rock. The peak is a long way from Colin Todd Hut and requires a bivvy, perhaps on the north side of the West Ridge of Stargazer.

6.10 North Ridge.

First ascent of the North Ridge appears to have been made by Conway Powell and Russell Falconer on November 19, 1969.

LESSER PEAKS OF THE BONAR GLACIER

Mt French (2356m)

7.1 The West Face. Grade 1+

Follow the Breakaway route from French Ridge Hut across the West Face towards the Bonar until either the first or second ramp above the Quarterdeck can be climbed to the summit ridge. The climb would take three to four hours from the hut.

➠ This route is subject to summer avalanches.

7.2 From the Bonar Glacier. Grade 1

From the top of the Quarterdeck traverse north-west along an easy snow ridge. Alternatively follow down the Bonar, striking up on to the ridge at any convenient point. Time, from French Ridge Hut to the summit, is about three hours. *Frank Wright, Dec 1914.*

Joffre (2091m)

7.3 From the Bonar Glacier. Grade 1

From the Bonar, Joffre is half an hour's easy rock scramble up any convenient route.

First ascent by a party led by Frank Wright, Dec 1914

7.4 The South Face. From Cannibalism to Karaoke. Grade 3+ (16)

From the head of the Matukituki Valley the South Face of Joffre is more involved than a half hour scramble. From near Scotts Bivvy head up to the face which is on the true right of the Breakaway. A steep spur just to the right of the avalanche gut carved by the Breakaway gives easy access to the face. The first ascent took a line which starts off a large patch of snow under an overhanging wall. Then taking the line of least resistance, climbed on a rising traverse which took in a series of ledges to come out near the top of the true right of the large gully that runs on a diagonal from the base of the face to the summit.

There are approximately 10 pitches and, of these, half are good rock. It would be possible to construct a more pleasant line by the use of bolts and taking a more direct line to the summit.
Geoff Ellis & Allan Uren, Jan 1999.

After topping out on the first ascent, to a perfect summers evening, the two climbers wandered down the Bonar to Colin Todd Hut in running shoes. Like a couple of street kids they threw themselves on the mercy of the residents and passed a pleasant night with borrowed food and a blanket. Camaraderie and hospitality are still alive and well in the hills—may it always be so.

➠ The slopes above the face are subject to avalanches.

Bevan (2030m)

Bevan is not so much a climb as a glorious viewpoint. Still it is in the greater alps and not to be taken lightly. It was the scene of one of the most protracted and gruelling rescues in the region, a five day ordeal for a dozen men trapped on Bevan Col. The whole story can be read in the classic book *Men Aspiring* by Paul Powell.

The peak was first climbed by Dennis Leigh, Bill Walker, and Jock Sim, who filled in the rest of their afternoon after their first ascent of Avalanche on December 28, 1939 by racing down the Bonar to Bevan Col and on to Bevan, before returning to French Ridge via the Quarterdeck that evening.

7.5 From Bevan Col. Grade 1

From Bevan Col easy snow and broken rock slopes lead direct to the summit. Tempting ledges leading around on to the North Face terminate on exposed rock and should be avoided by parties more interested in the view. The climb is unlikely to take more than an hour from the col.

7.6 The North Ridge. Grade 1+

The ridge is gained from gravelly ledges leading up from the Bonar just above the icefall. Then a slabby ridge is followed which is straightforward although quite exposed, with a few small towers towards the top. The ridge takes about two hours, with five hours being necessary for the round trip from Colin Todd Hut.

Conway Powell & Russell Falconer, Nov 1969.

7.7 The South West Ridge. Grade 1

From Hector Col the South West Ridge is a straightforward mixed rock and snow climb, probably requiring about two hours from the col to the summit. Hector Col is reached using the Bevan Col route (A12).

Jock & Peter Sim, Jack Kerr & Ian Johnstone, Dec 1939.

South Face of Joffre in summer showing route 7.4, *From Cannabalism to Karaoke.* The dip on the right is the Breakaway. *Allan Uren.*

7.4

POPE'S NOSE (2700M)

8.1 From the Bonar Glacier. Grade 2

This small peak is a great vantage point and has a stomach sucking drop down the East Face. It is an exposed straightforward climb from the Bonar Glacier. A short climb up steep snow slopes beneath and between the two peaks, then an airy traverse eastwards along the ridge. About five hours from French Ridge Hut.

Harry Stevenson, Doug Dick & David Lewis, Dec 1936.

8.2 The North East Ridge. Grade 3

Although the North East Ridge is steep, clean-cut, and appealing, it was not attempted until 1969, when it was climbed by Laurie Kennedy and Dave Innes.

The ridge is gained from Moncrieff Col by following routes A19 and A24 to the upper shelf of the Volta Glacier. Continue up the snow until underneath the peak and following a sloping ledge back out to the south west to gain the ridge at the foot of the steep section. From here the climbing is sustained about grade 14-15 with wild exposure down the East Face. The rock is good, with an easier section high on the ridge followed by another short steep section immediately below the summit. The climb requires about six hours from Moncrieff Col to the peak. It is also possible to access the Volta from the Bonar by descending down between the two peaks of Pope's Nose. Two rappels may be required. This route is only practicable if a large snow ramp is formed on the north side.

Laurie Kennedy & Dave Innes, Feb 1969.

The East Face

8.3 F*** The Pope. Grade 6+

The East Face is a fantastic sweep of compact dark schist with small roofs which lend it an air of impregnability. During winter this air hangs heavily around the face and lines of ice contribute to give it an unfriendly persona. This is what Nick Cradock, Brian Alder, Dave Fearnley and Lionel Clay were hoping to sample when they made the first ascent, during winter, of the face. The face had been attempted before by Nick and various partners, but they were thwarted by a lack of good ice. This seems to be a characteristic of the face. The first, and subsequent ascent parties have used a helicopter to access this very isolated place. A challenge still exists for a party to walk in and climb—a committing prospect. As of the printing of this guide the face has not been repeated in winter.

This 18 pitch route is steepest in the lower section and weaves around linking up the runnels. With fatter ice it would be possible to take a more direct line. The first ascent party bivvied and, unless good conditions are encountered, a bivvy for successive parties will also be required because of the size of the route and short winter days.

Nick Cradock, Brian Alder, Dave Fearnley & Lionel Clay, July/Aug 1990.

Dave Vass beneath the Kitchener Cirque, East Face of Pope's Nose, Winter. *Allan Uren.*

Rotten rock tower

8.3

8.5

8.4

East Face of Pope's Nose. Winter conditions. Edge of Bonar Glacier at top left. *Allan Uren.*

8.4 Bishop's Buttress. Grade 5 (17)

During summer the face is usually free of ice and good clean rock prevails. In the summer of 1999 Dave Vass, Richard Turner, Allan Uren and Clinton Beavan made the first summer ascents via different routes. Helicopter access was used.

Bishop's Buttress is the buttress on the left side of the face and tops out on the Bonar Glacier, not the summit of Pope's Nose. The first 8 or 9 pitches are up a corner system of perfect rock at grade 17. A standard rock rack was used. After a prominent tower the rock deteriorates, but could possibly be better if instead of going to the tower you trend right up a steep wall. The last four pitches are of poor rock and care is required not to end up on *bird-brain boulevard*.
Allan Uren and Clinton Beavan, summer 1999.

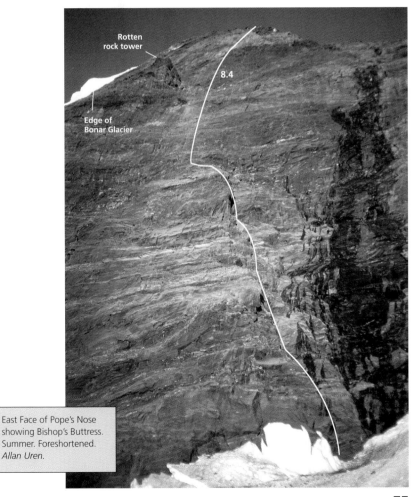

Rotten
rock tower

8.4

Edge of
Bonar Glacier

East Face of Pope's Nose
showing Bishop's Buttress.
Summer. Foreshortened.
Allan Uren.

8.5 **The Vision. Grade 5 (20)**

This is a fine line up the centre of the face on steep solid rock. Twelve technical pitches and then some scrambling to the Bonar Glacier.
Dave Vass, Richard Turner, summer 1999.

➠ It should be noted that despite the ease of access with a helicopter the Upper Kitchener Cirque is an isolated place and to escape from it in a storm would be a serious proposition, not joking.

RIGHT. Clinton Beavan leading on the first ascent of *Bishop's Buttress*. East Face of Pope's Nose. *Allan Uren.*

AVALANCHE (2606M)

A valanche is a very attractive mountain, especially as seen from French Ridge. It offers a variety of routes, several of which are 'on' in a relatively short day from the hut or if the weather is looking doubtful.

9.1 The North Ridge. Grade 3

The first party on the North Ridge consisted of Neil Hamilton, Pearl Wright and Ron Knightley, who descended it on January 4, 1949, during the first traverse of the mountain. The first ascent appears to have been made unknowingly by David Somerset and Tom Carter on January 9, 1956.

The ridge is reached from the head of the Bonar Glacier. Most parties, seeking protection from the weather, have climbed on very exposed ledges on the Kitchener side, however, the crest of the ridge or the western slabs may be more desirable in good conditions. Two prominent steps occur. The first is low on the ridge and can apparently be negotiated on either side, but the upper one is turned by ledges on the east. The ridge takes 3 to 4 hours from the head of the glacier or 6 to 7 hours from French Ridge Hut.

9.2 The West Ridge. Grade 2 (10)

Climb to the Bonar via the Quarterdeck and continue up the glacier on the north side of the ridge to avoid the gendarmes of the lower section. Gain the ridge at the foot of the slabs. Although some of the rock is loose, the slabs offer pleasant climbing (approx. rock grade 10) and lead directly to the West (highest) Peak. The time necessary from the hut to the summit is usually between 4 to 6 hours.

Dennis Leigh, Bill Walker & Jock Sim, Jan 1935.

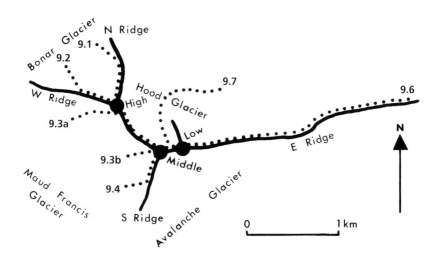

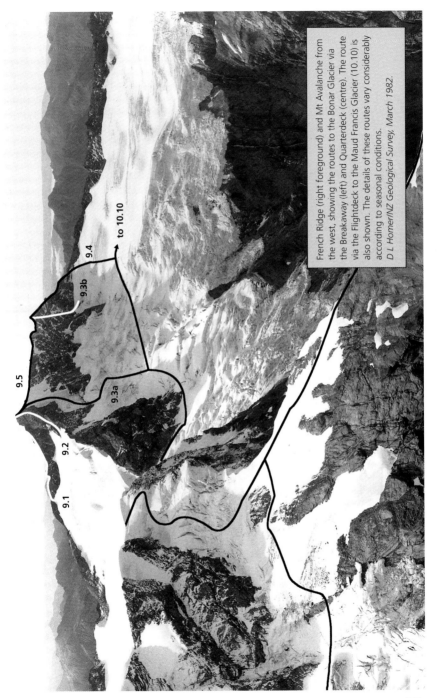

French Ridge (right foreground) and Mt Avalanche from the west, showing the routes to the Bonar Glacier via the Breakaway (left) and Quarterdeck (centre). The route via the Flightdeck to the Maud Francis Glacier (10.10) is also shown. The details of these routes vary considerably according to seasonal conditions.
D L Homer/NZ Geological Survey, March 1982.

9.3 The South West Face

Two rather similar routes give predominantly snow climbs: 9.3a to the West Peak and 9.3b to the Middle Peak. The route to the West Peak was first climbed by Jim Riley and Sid Lane on November 24, 1958 and 9.3b was descended by Tony Bowden and Graham Bishop in 1963, after their climb of the South Ridge.

9.3a Grade 2+

From the Maud Francis Glacier (see route 9.4) cross the schrund to reach the steep snow ramp leading up below but parallel to the slabs of the West Ridge. The ramp joins the summit ridge just east of the West Peak. This route has been skied.

9.3b Grade 2

A less prominent, and less steep, snow lead rises from the Maud Francis Glacier almost directly below the notch of the summit ridge. The snow runs out about 30 metres below the middle peak and the climb is completed on the easy rock of the South Ridge. Late in the season this route may be almost clear of snow and may be followed on easy slabs.

9.4 The South Ridge. Grade 2

The South Ridge leads directly to the Middle Peak. Climb the Quarterdeck to the Bonar and descend the Flightdeck to reach the Maud Francis Glacier. The rock of the South Ridge is reached from a snow lead where the ridge begins to steepen towards the peak.

During the first ascent most of the climbing was done on the steep loose rock of the eastern side of the ridge in order to escape the wind but in better conditions the slabby western side may be found easier. The prominent tower about halfway up is turned on the west. The first ascent was made in 5 hours from Colin Todd Hut and the climb would probably take a similar time from French Ridge.

To traverse to the East Peak requires only a few minutes along an easy ridge. The traverse to the West Peak has not been made in this direction, but would probably involve rappelling into the notch.
Tony Bowden & Graham Bishop, Jan 1963.

9.5 Traverse from West to East Peak. Grade 4

The traverse of the summit ridge is a far more exacting proposition than the West Ridge. The crux of the traverse is a deep notch, which requires a very delicate descent of a forty metre wall and an even more difficult climb out the other side. Kennedy and Innes took seven hours from the west to the middle peak, of which three were spent getting past the notch.

The ridge from the middle to the East Peak is straightforward and normally requires only a few minutes. This route has probably not had a second ascent.
Laurie Kennedy & Dave Innes, Feb 1969.

Avalanche (East Peak, 2533m)

The East Ridge and East Peak of Avalanche dominate the view from the road up the Matukiktuki Valley. They also dominated Paul Powell's climbing intentions for six years until October 23, 1960, when with Don McTaggart, Bob Cunninghame and Geoff Bayliss, he finally succeeded with a route from the Hood Glacier.

9.6 The East Ridge. Grade 4

Climb to the col west of Duncan's Knob, either from Glacier Burn or Aspiring Flat. The ridge is then followed, with some minor digressions on the north side to turn some of the early bumps. A difficult step about 70m high occurs just past a sharp bend in the ridge; beyond this the ridge is a mixture of very easy sections on loose rock and more demanding climbing on the steeper sections, until the col at the foot of the final step below the peak is reached. This step has been climbed by a difficult chimney on the north east side, but easier ledges with good holds are present on the Avalanche Glacier side.

The first ascent, from a bivvy near the col at the end of the ridge, required about nine hours to the summit.

Bruce Robertson & Dave Innes. Easter, 1969.

9.7 Via the Hood Glacier. Grade 2+

Use access route A18 to access the Hood Glacier. From the head of the névé a short but steep rock climb leads to the summit ridge between the east and the middle peaks. The rock notch can also be reached from the col between Duncan's Knob and the East Ridge (approached either from Aspiring Flat or Glacier Burn), by sidling the first knob of the ridge on the north side on an exposed deer trail, and then traversing, on a gradual descent, the snowgrass ledges and snow on the north side of the ridge.

The climb would require a bivvy above the bushline.

Don McTaggart, Bob Cunninghame & Geoff Bayliss, Oct 1960.

ROB ROY (2644M)

Rob Roy is a mountain pushed up by the tectonic plates and in the process given multiple birth defects. Ridges and faces don't come together with the symmetry of Aspiring and climbers shy away from the hunch-backed summit. Despite appearances however, the mountain has a magnetism and a wonderful array of varied and interesting routes.

The first ascent, from the West Matukituki and the Rob Roy Glacier, was on March 2, 1935, when the mountain was overwhelmed by the sheer weight of numbers of a party consisting of Ernie Smith, Monty McClymont, Cedric Benzoni, Bob Fullerton, George Palmer, Don Divers, Russell Edwards, George Edwards, and Gordon Edwards, via route 10.6.

Access to head of Rob Roy Stream and climbing routes.

Above the bushline continue on the true left bank of Rob Roy Stream through light scrub and tussock, keeping 100m above the stream. After crossing a washed-out stream bed follow around terraces until a small silty flat is reached. From here find a convenient place to descend to the avalanche-threatened Rob Roy Glacier.

During the summer the avalanche hazard comes from the glaciers above and in the winter from large gullies dropping from Homestead Peak. A broad spur to the left of the large gully dropping from Homestead Peak is then climbed which ends up merging with the snowfield underneath the Homestead Peak and Rob Roy Col.

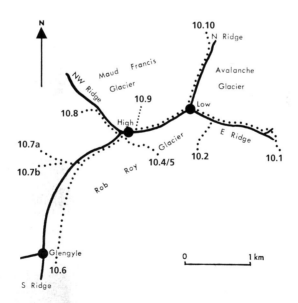

LEFT: Looking up Rob Roy Stream to the South Face and East Ridge of Rob Roy. *Geoff Wayatt/Mountain Recreation.*

10.1 **The East Ridge. Grade 3+**

Although tantalising glimpses of the East Ridge can be seen from the West Matukituki it was not until January 10, 1963, that the ridge was climbed, when Tony Bowden and Graham Bishop traversed the mountain from a bivvy at the head of Rob Roy Stream.

The ridge rises from the Homestead-Rob Roy Col in two prominent steps. The lower one forms a triangular face with the snow shelf beneath giving access to the Avalanche Glacier. The route traverses this shelf to a point from which the north edge of the triangular face can be gained. This edge provides enjoyable climbing on steep rock, but it could be avoided by traversing the ledge further towards the Avalanche Glacier, where a snow route allows a return to the ridge above the first step.

There is a variation on the left side of the first rock step up an ill defined gully involving grade 15 rockclimbing on sound rock. The second step, although loose and exposed, is straightforward, as is the rest of the mixed rock and snow ridge to the Low Peak, about five hours from the col. The traverse to the High Peak commences with a gentle descent on an easy snow arête until the ridge is blocked by a large gendarme. This is turned on the west side and beyond it 100-200 metres of exposed but technically straightforward rock lead to the snow cone of the high peak, two to three hours from the low peak. Slings and pitons would be the protection of choice for the traverse.

The traverse from the foot of the East Ridge to Aspiring Hut via the High Peak and route 10.7a has been completed in 13 hours.

Tony Bowden & Graham Bishop, Jan 1963.

The South Face

After reaching the col there are a number of options to gain the foot of the South Face. These options have come into being because of the great glacial recession.

(1) Climb most of the way up the ridge separating the Little South Face (the Little South Face is the triangular face with the East Ridge on its right hand edge) and the South Face then descend to the glacier. Be aware that the small ice cliff clinging to the face down and right of the Low peak is active and deposits debris all the way down to the lower glacier.

(2) The Little South Face has a number of interesting gully lines on it which give a challenging start at about grade 4.

(3) Climb the East Ridge to the top of the second step avoiding the first rock step and descend route 10.2.

10.2 **The South East Corner. Grade 2**

This route is very difficult to access due to the 'great glacial recession'. This route has become more of a way of accessing the South Face than a climb. The South East corner is a fifty five degree, prominent snow and ice tongue leading

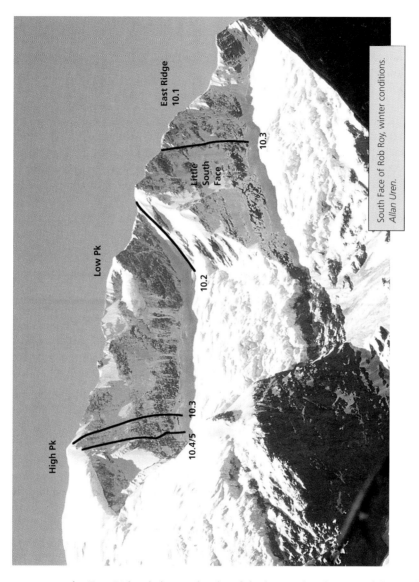

South Face of Rob Roy, winter conditions.
Allan Uren.

up to the East Ridge, below and right of the low peak. The route follows the snow and ice leads, with a steeper section of about 150 metres of rock in the middle, before more snow leads out to the ridge about 100 metres below the low peak. In the winter this is all snow. This was used as the access route to the upper névé for the ascent of the South Face route 10.3. Moore's time from the névé to the ridge was about one hour.
Pete Moore, early Dec 1972.

10.3 A Couple Of Days. Grade 5+

This is an all ice route climbed in late winter. A gully on the Little South Face was climbed, 10 pitches of grade 4 and then route 10.2 was descended into the upper névé to access the main South Face. The route on the South Face takes a series of ill defined gullies right of the summer route. After about 6 pitches there is a sixty five degree snowslope, 2 pitches. Three pitches from the summit a steep rock corner is climbed on ice with good rock protection. This leads onto a steep arête then up a gully and onto the summit snow slopes finishing just right of the summit. Sixty metre ropes were used. Three bivvies were had, one at the base of the Little South Face, another in the bergschrund at the bottom of the South Face and one on the Maud Francis Glacier.
Dave Vass & Allan Uren, Sept 1997.

10.4 The Zone. Grade 5

"Ok, so if Craig peels off making this move over that bulge, that piton's gonna pull along with the stake right out of this manky snow. Which leaves Craig, Gareth and I fast accelerating to the glacier two hundred metres below. "Yeah Man you're looking solid. Charge it!"

So the dialogue went between the lads trying to access the South Face via the ridge bisecting the Little South Face and route 10.2. They managed not to fall off and went on to climb a route on the South Face between the original summer route and *A Couple of Days,* finishing as for the summer route. The lower part of the route was sustained steep ice. Overall length 9 pitches.
Craig Jefferies, Steve Moffat & Gareth Sharp, June 1999.

10.5 The South Face Original Line. Grade 5

The route on the face follows the well-defined rib that falls from right to left from the summit. Two broad gullies lying to the left of this rib are swept frequently by ice avalanches from the cliffs above. Cross the schrund to the right of the foot of the rib. The foot of the rib is very steep and it is climbed on its eastern flank, where about 300 metres of fairly sustained rock climbing leads to the crest. Steep snow and ice (rock later in the summer) provide straightforward climbing for the next 300 metres. A small overhang on the rib is climbed directly, beyond which steep ice patches lead to the final snow and ice slopes beneath the summit. The initial party, with a rope of three, spent about 10 hours on the face.
Bob Cunninghame, Limbo Thompson & Pete Glasson. Dec 1972.

10.6 The South Ridge and Rob Roy Glacier. Grade 2

Across the Matukituki and slightly downstream from Wilson's Camp there is a large avalanche gully which in winters of high snow fall deposits debris in the valley floor. This gully gives fast and unimpeded travel to above the bush line. There is a small waterfall at the bottom but this is easily negotiated on the true left on a deer trail. Most parties attempting this route have bivvied at 1600 metres, before crossing the ridge to gain the broad crevassed snowfields of the

Craig Jefferies hanging
out at the top of the
first pitch. *The Zone*,
South Face of Rob Roy.
Gareth Sharp.

Rob Roy Glacier. These provide a straightforward route, on a rising traverse, to the high peak.

➠ Note. There may be a large schrund below the summit. The climb can take 10–11 hours from the valley floor and is a comfortable weekend trip from the Raspberry Flat carpark. The round trip from carpark to carpark taking in the High Peak-Low Peak traverse and down the Rob Roy stream has been accomplished during one long hot summers day.

E Smith, M McClymont, C Benzoni, B Fullerton, G Palmer, D Divers, R Edwards, G Edwards & G Edwards, March 1935.

87

10.7 **The West Face. Grade 2+**

The West Face was initially descended by Paul Powell and Frank Cooper in 1954, and again by Tony Bowden and Graham Bishop in 1963. The first ascent was not until 1964 when Don Morrison and Peter Child climbed it from Shovel Flat.

Four variations are available on the face: 10.7a–d

10.7a **Grade 2+**

From Aspiring Hut cross to the east bank of the Matukituki and from the head of the flats climb through the bush into the tussock and snow basins above. The ice cliffs of a small hanging glacier, visible from the hut, are turned on the east, before easy snow and finally slabby rock lead out to the South Ridge about one kilometre south of the High Peak.
Don Morrison & Peter Child. 1964.

10.7b **Grade 2+**

Use route A5 described in the access route section to access the face from Shovel Flat. The rib to the north is crossed at an easy col (1950m) and is then followed up on snowfields on the north side. Access to the steeper upper snowfield may be complicated by a short rock step. The rib eventually merges into the face, from which point steep but easy slabs lead out to the summit ridge about one kilometre south of the High Peak. Both this and the previous route are long climbs from the valley floor and would probably be more enjoyable from a camp above the bushline.

10.7c **Grade 2+**

A steep, broad gully splits the face offering eight to ten pitches of excellent snow climbing. Subject to mid-summer slab avalanches. It is a mixed climb in the late summer.

10.7d **Grade 2+**

Climb steep snow for three pitches, followed by three moderate pitches to a gap in the South West Ridge. Then cross to the top of a hanging glacier to meet the previous route (10.7c).

10.8 **The North West Ridge. Grade 2+**

Follow route 10.7b to the col on the rib running down from the West Face. The snowfields to the north are easily traversed, climbing steadily towards a prominent col on the North West Ridge. Above the latter col the ridge is steep and slabby but consists of sound rock. The first two or three pitches are the most difficult and involve two awkward steps, both of which are turned over the Maud Francis Glacier. Above them the angle eases and the remainder of the ridge is straightforward rock and snow, leading to the summit ridge about 150m south of the high peak. The climb takes about five hours from the col on the rib from the West Face to the summit.
Laurie Kennedy and Graham Bishop, Dec 1973.

10.8

10.9

To Bonar Glacier

Maud Francis Glacier

10.7a

10.7b

10.7c

10.7d

Western aspect of Rob Roy viewed across Gloomy Gorge from French Ridge Hut.
Geoff Wayatt/Mountain Recreation.

10.9 The North Face. Grade 3

The expanse of the North Face dominates the view of Rob Roy from French Ridge. Although tantalisingly close across the slot of Gloomy Gorge, the only practicable access is via the Maud Francis Glacier (see route 10.10). Follow route 10.10 across the upper slopes of the Maud Francis Glacier and continue until more or less beneath the High Peak. Access to the face is by a prominent snow chute, above which snow and ice leads are followed to reach the summit ridge about 50 metres north of the High Peak. The nature of the route can vary considerably depending on conditions. The first party took about two hours from the névé to the summit.

Bruce Robertson and Laurie Kennedy, Dec 1975.

10.10 The North Ridge. Grade 3+

The North Ridge leads to the Low Peak (2609m) which is separated by a long airy summit ridge from the High Peak (2644m).

From French Ridge climb the Quarterdeck to the Bonar and then descend the Flightdeck to reach the Maud Francis Glacier. Cross the névé to gain the North Ridge where it begins to steepen towards the Low Peak and follow the crest to the summit. Time from the hut to the summit is about nine hours.

First ascent and first traverse to High Peak; Paul Powell & Frank Cooper, Dec 1954.

10.11 The North East Face.

The North East Face above the Avalanche Glacier appears to be a straightforward snow route and can be reached either from the head of Rob Roy Stream (see route 10.1) or from French Ridge by crossing the divide between the Maud Francis and Avalanche Glaciers at its lowest point. It has potential as a rapid escape route from Low Peak.

10.12 Bonar Glacier-Rob Roy Stream traverse. Grade 2

This traverse, taking in the Maud Francis and Avalanche Glaciers and Rob Roy Stream is a way of walking out from climbing in the Mt Aspiring region and avoiding the walk down the Matukituki Valley. From the Bonar descend the Flightdeck and traverse around the Maud Francis and cross the ridge between Mt Avalanche and Rob Roy near the middle. Then continue down and around the Avalanche Glacier and link up with the snow shelf which runs underneath the East Ridge of Rob Roy. Use the access route for the head of Rob Roy Stream in reverse from the Rob Roy-Homestead col. The Avalanche Glacier may be a tangle of decomposed ice near the end of the summer and require more time than advised. Usual times are: Bonar to Homestead Col, 6–8 hours and Homestead Col to carpark, 4–5 hours.

10.13 The South West Ridge. Grade 3 (14)

This route climbs the South West Ridge to the pyramid peak east of the low peak. Steep rock (iced or grade 14) followed by a snow arête.

Phil Penney & Simon Harris, Nov 1998.

CLIMBS FROM ASPIRING FLAT

Aeroplane (2340m)

11.1 The South Buttress. Grade 3

The South Buttress is reached by traversing across from the Moncrieff Col route and then following directly up snow and shattered rock just west of the crest of the middle rib.

Bruce Robertson and Laurie Kennedy, Jan 1975.

Moncrieff (2262m)

The first ascent of Moncrieff (originally named Mercer) was made on January 4, 1959, by Garth Matterson, Don Mee and Dove Tarrant, from Moncrieff Col.

11.2 The South Face. Grade 2+

Follow the Moncrieff Col route from Aspiring Flat to reach the snowfield below the col. Traverse north to reach the rib separating the Kitchener and Lucas Glaciers. This rib leads to a steep snowfield below the South Face, which is then climbed by a direct line to the summit. The rock is unpleasantly loose but otherwise not unduly difficult.

This is a very long climb from Aspiring Flat, probably requiring eight to ten hours to the summit, but the reward is a magnificent view. There is a bivvy rock on the Moncrieff Col route. This bivvy is big enough for three people to stay dry in even in the most atrocious conditions. See A19.

Martyn Potter, Maurice Conway & Wayne McIlwraith, Jan 1970.

Sisyphus (1859m)

Sisyphus, although only a scramble in summer conditions, reigns supreme as the viewpoint of the East Matukituki. An incredible view of Mt Aspiring and all the other big peaks is the prize for climbing this peak. There are three main approaches, the best one being by the West Ridge via Wilmot Saddle and Rainbow Stream.

11.3 Via Wilmot Saddle. Grade 1

This is the recommended route. Follow up Rainbow Stream from Aspiring Flat to where scree and scrub slopes lead up to Wilmot Saddle (1680m). Stay on the true left of Rainbow Stream until the slopes below Wilmot Saddle ease in steepness. From the saddle follow the West Ridge to the summit.

Rainbow Valley, like most of the valleys of the area, is subject to avalanche danger in the spring and early summer.

Eric Miller, Howard Boddy, Jim Shanks & Robert Pinney, Dec 1930.

Aerial view above Aspiring Flat. Kitchener River (left). Route marked in gray is access to the Volta Glacier via Moncrieff Col. ➠ See also photo on page 30. *Colin Monteath/Hedgehog House.*

Moncrieff Col

11.1

Aspiring

8.2

Pope's Nose

11.4 The South Ridge. Grade 1+

From Aspiring Flat climb through bush and scrub from near the Rainbow-Kitchener confluence to gain the South Ridge which may then be followed to the summit. See the route identified on page 82 of *Moir's Guide North* to avoid considerable scrub-bashing.

CLIMBS FROM JUNCTION FLAT

Dragonfly Peak (2165m)

The name, one of several in the East Maukituki with aeronautical connotations, commemorates a Dragonfly aircraft that went missing without trace, possibly in the Mount Aspiring area in 1962. The first recorded ascent of the peak was made by Paul Powell and Bruce Moore in March 1962, from the South Albertburn Saddle.

11.5 The North Ridge. Grade 1

From Junction Flat cross the East Matukituki and follow the marked track up through the bush on the north side of Hester Pinney Creek. Above the bush easy tussock slopes lead around to the South Albertburn Saddle. From the saddle follow the straightforward tussock and rock of the North Ridge to the summit. This would take about seven to eight hours from the river.

CLIMBS FROM RUTH FLAT

Aspinall (1908m)

Howard Boddy, the pioneer of the East Matukituki, made the first ascent of Aspinall with his brother, Ernie, in February 1930.

11.6 The South West Ridge. Grade 1

Continue up the East Matukituki until near the foot of the waterfall, where a ridge leads North East directly to the summit. The scrub can be avoided by climbing up a small creek bed on the south side of the ridge, the crest of which then provides a straightforward route to the peak. Snow faces on the south side of the ridge allow some gaps and towers to be bypassed. The summit rocks are most easily climbed on the north side. The climb takes about seven hours from Ruth Flat to the summit.

Glacier Dome (2387m)

Glacier Dome has the distinction of being the first mountain in the area to be climbed as a recreational exercise. Admittedly Ebenezer Teichelmann, Alec Graham and Jack Clarke had higher aspirations in 1908, but they found their time exhausted after their long journey up the Waiatoto River. On February 1 they climbed a leading ridge north of the Volta icefall to reach a rocky peak (2015 m) above the névé. Descending to the glacier they then crossed over to the easy slopes of Glacier Dome, from where they admired Aspiring, their elusive objective.

11.7 Via Ruth Ridge. Grade 2+

Climb Ruth Ridge (A22) and cross the Volta to the straightforward snow slopes leading to the summit of Glacier Dome, five to six hours from Ruth Flat.
➠ Note: Getting onto the Volta may be problematic at times, e.g. late summer, due to a steep broken section.

Lois (1981m)

Lois was first climbed by Howard Boddy and Jack Foster in February 1933.

11.8 Ridge from Rabbit Pass. Grade 1

Climb to the shelf above the waterfall at the head of the East Matukituki. A broad easy ridge leads eastwards to the summit, about one hour from the point where the shelf is reached and four to five hours from Ruth Flat.
➠ Note: This is not the peak of Lois marked on the metric topo map, the Lois metric map point is further on and more tricky).

Sisyphus (1859m)

11.9 The North East slopes. Grade 1

From Ruth Flat climb the bush and tussock slopes on the north-east flank of the peak. The slopes directly below Wilmot Saddle are subject to stonefall and should be avoided.

Ruth Flat

Pickelhaube

RUTH RIDGE

Lois

Aspinall

Ruth Flat and the head of the East Matukituki. Ruth Ridge (left) and the East Matukituki-Wilkin Saddle routes are marked. *D G Bishop, March 1959.*

95

Tantalus Rock (1951m)

Originally called Gehenna Rock, Tantalus Rock was first climbed by Paul Powell and Peter Child on January 10, 1965.

11.10 Via Ruth Ridge. Grade 2+

From the top of Ruth Ridge, Tantalus Rock is but a few minutes easy scramble above the Volta Névé. It would probably take about five hours from Ruth Flat to the summit.

FASTNESS (2383M)

To gaze up at the East Face from Ruth Flat… 'a great featureless rock wall rising 1000m with no lines, no cracks, no ledges' and the reason for the name is clear.

No less awesome today than how it was perceived fifty years ago, the East Face of Fastness has proven to be a little shorter at 750m and there are cracks and ledges. But the climbing is as awesome as it was originally perceived to be, as Peter Dickson and his Polish partner, Miroslavc Sveticic found out when they made the first ascent in 1990. The pair accessed the face directly from Ruth Flat up the waterfall issuing from the face. In Peter's understated comment *'It's not a good way to get there'*, he sums up how well defended the face is.

The West Ridge of Fastness and first ascent of the peak was completed by Paul Powell, Colin Marshall, John Sage and Earle Riddiford in Dec 1945 from a camp on the Volta Glacier. Twenty years later Paul Powell was again camped on the Volta, this time to make the first ascent of the North Ridge with Keith Skinner, Peter Child and Geoff Bayliss on January 2, 1965.

The South Ridge was first ascended by Garth Matterson, Don Mee and Dave Tarrant on January 4, 1959. The mountain, and in particular the East Face, has everything the modern alpinist could wish for and will always deliver an intense experience.

12.1 The West Ridge. Grade 2

From the Volta Névé there are several snow and rock leads on the north side of the ridge which give good access to the rock at the top of the West Ridge. An overhang near the top of the ridge can be avoided by moving out onto the snowfield on the south side and a snow route is then followed to the summit. Time from névé to summit is about 3 hours.
Paul Powell, Colin Marshall, John Sage & Earle Riddiford, Dec 1945.

12.2 The North Ridge. Grade 2+

The first 300m are steep and are climbed by a series of steep and loose rock couloirs, with some difficult pitches towards the top. The angle then eases and a long section can be turned on easy snow on the west side, before a final short, steep rock pitch leads to the summit.
Paul Powell, Keith Skinner, Peter Child & Geoff Bayliss, Jan 1965.

12.3 The South Ridge. Grade 2

The South Ridge is a straightforward rock ridge rising from the Volta Glacier near Rainbow Col. This col is not accessible from the east. To descend the South Ridge to Moncrieff Col would take about 3 hours.
Garth Matterson, Don Mee & Dave Tarrant, Jan 1959.

12.4 The East Ridge. Grade 3+

The ridge rises steeply for about 400m in a series of buttresses from the west end of Wilmot Saddle. The rock is generally poor, and is muddy and vegetated on the East Face side. Belay points are found using pitons and a good selection are recommended for this route. The ridge was also descended after the first winter ascent using two 60m ropes and pitons. Normal descent routes available are via Moncrieff Col or Ruth Ridge.

Gain the foot of the ridge from Wilmot Saddle or by steep gullies leading to a prominent notch at the foot of the ridge. When there is sufficient snow the gully option is the best. The first buttress is good rock and may be climbed direct; thereafter the crest of the ridge is followed where practicable until the angle eases and either the ridge or a snow route on the South Face can be followed to the summit. Although the first buttress is the most technically demanding part of the climb, the first party considered a very steep, poorly protected pitch of mud and rubbish necessary to bypass the third step, as the crux. It may be possible to bypass this pitch by continuing straight up the buttress, although this may be more technical.

Times. From Wilmot Saddle to the top of the steep section takes about four hours, with a further two hours to the summit. From the summit to Moncrieff Col requires about three hours.

Bruce Robertson and Laurie Kennedy, Jan 1974.

North East side of Aspiring

The East Ridge and East Face of Fastness, with Wilmot saddle in the left foreground. Late summer conditions. *D G Bishop.*

12.4

Fastness

East Face of Mt Fastness, winter conditions.
John Clyma.

12.5

12.6

East Ridge
descent route

Access to
face

12.5 East Face. Dickson/Sveticic. Grade 4+ (17).

Access to the East Face is via the Rainbow Valley and gullies on the south side of Wilmot Saddle to a notch at the base of the East Ridge. This notch leads down onto a large terrace that bisects the bottom of the face.

The East Face is a spectacular sweep of rock. The upper third is the steepest section. The first ascent of the face took a line up the centre, topping out close to the summit. The route starts on the right hand side of three faint pillars in the middle of the face. Careful route finding is required through these, at grade 16. It then carries on up to a pocketed slab on fantastic rock. This steepens and merges with the summit pyramid, grade 17. Dickson and Sveticic soloed most of the route, belaying only two pitches, in three and a half hours.

Other rock routes are possible on this huge face. Note the summit pyramid is not the summit, the real summit is several hundred metres to the west. Descent was down the North Ridge, scrambling down ledge systems to the big terrace that bisects the bottom of the face, an easy descent route.

Peter Dickson and Miroslavc Sveticic, March 1990.

12.6 East Face. Storming the Barbican. Grade 6+

This sixteen pitch winter route aims for a series of corners just left of the summit pyramid. The most difficult section is on the upper third of the face with two crux pitches of steep technical ice. At half height there is a large obvious steep gully which was avoided by traversing into the top from out left.

The first ascent party experienced an unplanned bivvy near the top of the face below the final crux, but this could have been avoided by an earlier start and climbing in the longer daylight hours of August. This crux was a pitch of near vertical chandelier water ice.

If the face is climbed in thin conditions, short snowstakes, pitons and snargs to bash, weld and coax into the mountain would be better than a rack of shiny titanium ice screws, although these would still come in handy. The face seems to form up between June and September. After September, because of the low altitude and sunny aspect, the ice on the face probably self-destructs.

Clinton Beavan, Al Wood & Allan Uren, July 1997.

CLIMBS FROM THE VOLTA NEVE

Aeroplane (2340m)

This name, along with Parachute Pass, commemorates an early and ill-fated experiment in the air dropping of supplies to a mountaineering party in the Kitchener Cirque in 1933. The peak was first climbed by Graham Bishop and Roger Barrowclough on December 27, 1961, from a camp on Moncrieff Col.

13.1 The North Face. Grade 2

The North Face is a short rock climb from the Volta Névé. The hardest pitches occur on sound rock leading out of the windscoop surrounding the peak and into the east side of a shallow gully. After 30–50m cross to the west side of this gully and climb out to the ridge, where easy loose rock leads to the summit. Time from the névé to the summit is 1–2 hours.

Graham Bishop & Roger Barrowclough, Dec 1961

13.2 The North East Ridge. Grade 2

The North East Ridge is a straightforward rock climb taking about one hour from the névé.

Laurie Kennedy & Dave Inne, Feb 1969.

Looking into the Volta Glacier from the top of Mt Aspiring, spring. *Duncan Ritchie.*

Aoraki/Mt Cook

Glacier Dome

Fastness

Volta Névé

Volta Glacier
Tom Hopkins/Hedgehog House.

Fastness

WAIATOTO

Glacier Dome

Charybdis (2367m)

13.3 **The West Ridge. Grade 2**

From Moncrieff Col traverse around the head of the Volta Névé beneath the ridge of the Main Divide before climbing about 100m of steep but easy rock to gain the upper shelf of the glacier. From the shelf good ledges lead up and east across the North Face of Scylla to give access to the col between Scylla and Charybdis. A short scramble on broken rock leads to the summit. The time to the top from Moncrieff Col is about five hours.

Graham Bishop, Roger Barrowclough & Henry Stoddart, after an abortive attempt on Scylla, Dec 1961.

Moncrieff (2282m)

13.4 **From Moncrieff Col. Grade 1+**

Moncrieff can be climbed in a few minutes by easy slabs north east of Moncrieff Col.

Scylla (2409m)

13.5 **The East Ridge. Grade 2+**

Follow route 13.3 until the col between Scylla and Charybdis is reached. The short ridge to the summit is barred by the crux of the climb, a difficult gendarme about 20m high, which is climbed direct. The climb takes about five hours from Moncrieff Col.

Laurie Kennedy & Dave Innes, Feb 1969.

NORTHERN MT ASPIRING NATIONAL PARK

I consider the name "Kuri" (the dog) for a not unattractive peak to be ill-chosen and unromantic, but there may be some justification for Awful and Dreadful. I am unaware who thought up these names, but they were given many years ago, at a time when these words had a meaning very different from their usage in the slang of today, and I feel they were given in all sincerity, the one solemnly impressive, inspiring awe; the other awe-inspiring. It is possible they have impressed to this degree those who have been privileged to look upon them.
— Eric Miller, 1945.

The mountains to the north of Mt Aspiring are fantastic. The approaches to Mt Alba, Castor, Pollux, and Mt Awful are a mirror image of the Aspiring peaks, in that they are approached up similar braided river valleys. However there are no alpine huts, or glaciers on the scale of the Volta or Bonar glaciers and most of the mountains are attempted from a bivvy. This is an area where trampers abound but mountaineers are thin on the ground.

Many of the smaller peaks have had very few ascents since they were first climbed. The peaks are generally grouped together around the valleys they are commonly climbed from. But because peaks are situated on the Main Divide, where ascents have been made from the west they are noted in the text.

Access

Road access to the mountains to the North of Mt Aspiring is via the Wanaka-Haast highway (6). Makarora township, eighty kilometres from Wanaka has a café, DoC centre and accommodation. Jet boat or plane access can be arranged for a quick trip to the Upper Wilkin Valley, jetboats at Makarora Tourist Centre, Makarora (03 443-8372) and a light plane can be used to fly into Jumboland, the Upper Wilkin and Siberia. See the listings at the rear of the book for more information.

The Wilkin and Young Valleys are tributaries of the Makarora and give access to Mts Alba, Awful, Castor and Pollux.

Northern Mt Aspiring huts

The valley huts that are present are owned and managed by DoC and a hut ticket or pass is necessary to stay in them. Alternatively, fees can be paid at any DoC office. Hut wardens are in attendance during the summer at Top Forks, Siberia and Young Huts.

Kerin Forks Hut

This hut can be found at the bush edge on the true right of the Wilkin River. It sleeps 10 and has a coal stove. 5–6 hours from the Makarora confluence.

Top Forks Hut

Located in the Upper Wilkin, beyond Jumboland Flat, Top Forks hut sleeps 10

LEFT. Kerie Carson on the upper slopes of Mt Pollux. Lake Castalia below. *Allan Uren.*

and has a coal stove. It provides access to Mts Castor and Pollux.

Siberia Hut

Siberia Hut sleeps 20 and has a potbelly stove. It is handily located near an airstrip and it is possible to fly directly in from Makarora, though this idea may be abhorrent to some. Siberia Hut provides a base for climbs of Mt Alba.

Young Hut

Situated near the bushline below Gillespie Pass in the Young Basin. Young Hut sleeps 10. Used as a base for climbs on Mt Awful.

CLIMBS FROM THE SOUTH WILKIN

Twilight (2127m)

14.1 Grade 1

Usually climbed via the leading spur that runs up from Waterfall Flat in the South Wilkin.

On the first ascent the ridge south of the peak was reached via a dry creek bed from the South Wilkin. The party descended the East Ridge to a point where it was possible to drop down through bush to the Wilkin Valley floor.

B Patterson, F Newmarch, H D Ombler, R Webster, Dec 1945.

Pickelhaube (2165m)

'Is it a new sauce invented to make rabbit stew more palatable?' mused Mr Explorer Charlie Douglas back in 1891. Ingenious but wrong, the name in fact refers to a distinctively shaped German helmet.

14.2 North East Ridge. Grade 2

Follow the ridge up from Pearson Saddle, for a time sidling on the Matukituki side until the ridge can be regained by a steep rock couloir. A mixed snow and rock ridge then leads up to the summit rocks with a final steep snow slope below the peak.

The climb would probably take about five hours from the saddle. The North East ridge could also be reached by the subsidiary ridge rising from the Wilkin-East Matukituki saddle.

Martin Lush, Ralph Markby, Cliff Anderson, Bill Brooks & Wilf Broughton, Dec 1948. Lush had made a solo ascent of the unamed peak (2105m) to the west a year earlier.

14.3 North West Ridge. Grade 2 (or 1+ from Volta)

The North West Ridge may be reached from Pearson Saddle by climbing scree and snow slopes to reach the ridge between Pickelhaube and the unnamed peak to the west. Although the ridge does not appear to have been climbed, it looks a straightforward rock ridge and would probably take about five hours from

Pearson Saddle. The ridge could also be reached without difficulty from the Volta Névé.

Taurus (2009m)

14.4 Grade 2

Climb to the prominent spur (exposed in parts) at the north end of Waterfall Flat, then cross the basin above to gain the northern slopes of Taurus.
B Paterson, R Webster, Jan 1946.

CLIMBS FROM THE NORTH WILKIN

Ragan (2254m)

The first ascent of Ragan was from the Waiatoto, via Razorback Ridge and across Stocking Peak by Charlie Douglas, February 1891.

15.1 Grade 1+

Climb to Chasm Pass, then along the Main Divide to summit.
A J McLeod, Jan 1946.

➠ Note: The grade given here is tentative as the route is seldom used.

Pollux (2536m)

Pollux is a fine mountain; the vertical relief is reminiscent of the Darran mountains. Top Forks Hut makes a great base, but may mean a long day and bivvying near the base of the mountain may be preferable.

15.2 Chasm Pass Route. Grade 2+

Climb to Chasm Pass and then cross the Ice King Tops and Donald Glacier to join the Bluffs route to the summit. The route of the first ascent, but rather long and indirect.
E Miller, J S Shanks, G B Thomas, A J Scott, W Young & J Dumbleton, Jan 1934.

15.3 Bluffs route. Grade 2+

This is the preferred route. From Top Forks Hut, take the track up the valley towards Lake Castalia and pick a line through alpine scrub up the ridge you can see from the hut and down from the lake. If time is taken and good route finding adhered to, the worst of the alpine scrub can be avoided. There is a steep gully to be negotiated before the glacier is reached from where the climbing is straightforward to the summit.
C C Benzoni, R R & G L Edwards, L W Divers & D C Peters, March 1937.

Helena Peak (2430m)

15.4 Grade 2+

Approached from North Wilkin (as with Bluffs Route) and climbed from the

col between it and Pollux.
H W Edwards, J F Foster, W E Wilson, Jan 1934.

Castor (2518m)

This fine, rarely climbed peak just to the north of Pollux offers better climbing than its neighbour.

15.5 Pickelhaube Glacier route. Grade 2+

Follow the Bluffs route on Pollux and traverse below Pollux into the Pickelhaube Glacier. From there the South West Face is straightforward.
The first ascent was made via Chasm Pass and the col between Pollux and Helena. C C Benzoni, L W Divers, R R & G L Edwards & D C Peters, March 1937.

15.6 East Ridge. Grade 3

From the top of the moraine wall between Lake Lucidus and the North Wilkin, pick a line through the bluffs to gain a shelf that leads out to the lower East Ridge. Follow the ridge to the summit.
Ian Baine & Graham McCallum. Dec 1963.

15.7 South East Face. Grade 2+

Gain the glacier above Lake Lucidus via the Bluffs route on Pollux. The route follows a prominent rock rib which merges into the snow of the face proper.
Margaret Fyfe & Graham McCallum, Jan 1975.

15.8 North West Ridge and Pickelhaube Glacier. Grade 2

From the Drake River sidle up the valley draining the Pickelhaube Glacier, to above bushline. Cut left up a scrub and tussock rib to slabs under Pegasus and follow benches to the Pickelhaube Glacier. Choose a route to suit up the last steeper bit.
Matt Warwick & Geoff Spearpoint, Feb 1979.

➠ **Note. Due to lack of information, grades have not been provided for many of the following routes.**

Pegasus (2160m)

15.9

Located at the end of the ridge that runs north-west from the summit of Castor. The pleasant slabs of the West Ridge have been climbed from the Drake valley. Use same access as described in 15.8.
T Barcham, B D Matthews & G J McCallum, Dec 1950.

Apollo (2124m)

15.10

Traverse from Mercury.
C Bentham, E Miller & S Turner, Jan 1929.

Mercury (2160m)

15.11

Climb out of the Lake Castalia Cirque, normally via Leda Peak route, and traverse upper snow slopes.
C Bentham, E Miller & S Turner, Jan 1929.

Leda (1546m)

15.12 Grade 1+

Climb slopes above Lake Castalia to saddle with Wonderland Valley. See *Moir's Guide North,* page 151.
C Bentham, E Miller & S Turner, Jan 1929.

Perseus (1815m)

15.13

From Top Forks, take the leading ridge. The ridge can also be gained via a prominent gully across the North Branch from Lake Diana. Perseus has also been climbed from the hanging valley to the east.
J D Hanning, Dec 1945.

Clio (1910m)

15.14

Climbed from Drake Valley.
A Cunningham & G J McCallum, Dec 1950.

Sombre (2040m)

15.15

East Face, from Drake Valley.
T Barcham, A Cunningham, B D Matthew & G J McCallum, Dec 1950.

Rosy (2093m)

15.16

Traverse ridge from Sombre.
T Barcham, A Cunningham, B D Matthew & G J McCallum, Dec 1950.

CLIMBS FROM JUMBOLAND

Jumbo (1945m)

16.1 **Grade 1**

Climb the spur at the head of Jumboland Flats. A magnificent viewpoint.
First recorded ascent N Begg, B Patterson & S Gilkison, Dec 1941.

Arne (2011m)

16.2 **South East Ridge.**

Just south of the Wonderland entrance, climb a boulder creek bed and through
bush to the ridge. Has also been climbed from the hanging valley to the west.
*J W Butchers, L Adkins, B Cahill, W E Wilson, W Hart, R Diedrich & J K Nicholls,
Dec 1929.*

Vesta (2027m)

16.3

Traverse the ridge from Arne.
H D Ombler, R Webster, Dec 1945.

Iphigenia (1994m)

16.4

Climb the ridge leading to the summit from the Wonderland Valley. On the
first ascent a snowcave was used—one of the first to be used in the New Zealand alps. Also climbed by traversing from Arne.
P & R Clark-Hall, Dec 1945.

Juno (2012m)

16.5 **North Ridge. Grade 2**

Ascended from bivvy near Lake Castalia. A steep rock scramble and traverse
down the south-west rock ledges.
*G Wayatt, J Muir, D Thomas, H Burr, T Barringer, A Burns, L Day, J Elwin, A
Brooks & C Buckland, Dec 1980.*

16.5a

Traverse from Iphigenia.
H D Ombler & R Webster, Dec 1945.

Oblong

16.6

From Jumboland, cross the Wilkin and take the creek to gain the ridge leading
up from the Wonderland.
H W Edwards, J F Foster & W E Wilson, Feb 1934.

Sentinel (1946m)

16.7 Grade 1+

Usually climbed as part of a traverse of the Main Divide from either Newland Pass or Lake Castalia.

Achilles (1890m)

16.8

Straightforward from Newland Pass, or along the Main Divide from The Sentinel.

Kuri (2141m)

16.9 North Ridge.

From Newland Valley, climb to the saddle north of the peak.
F Evison, R Jackson & R Oliver, Dec 1945.

Mt Alba (2360m)

16.10 South West Face. Grade 2

From Newland Pass at the head of Newland Stream, cross the Axius Glacier and climb the short, steep face to gain the summit ridge. For access to Newland Pass see *Moir's Guide North,* pages 93 and 151.
J D Knowles, A & G Edwards, L & A Divers, Dec 1939 (High Peak). T Barcham, A Cunningham, B D Matthews, G J McCallum, Dec 1950 (Middle and North Peaks).

16.11 East Ridge. Grade 2+

The Siberia is a hanging valley, a tributary of the Wilkin that has a friendly, isolated feeling. The recommended route is to go up the well formed track into the Crucible, a glacial lake trapped underneath the South East Face and, taking the line of least resistance, head up onto the East Ridge after which there is a snowfield and straightforward ridge to the top. It would be a long day from the hut and would possibly be best attempted from a bivvy near the Crucible. This route has had few ascents.

16.12 South East Face. Grade 2+

The South East Face has been climbed when Lake Crucible was frozen but it is not recommended as the face has a tendency to shed rocks and avalanches.
Phil Penney & Allan Uren, spring 1993.

16.13 North Face. Grade 2

Gain ledges below the East Ridge and traverse to reach a snowfield and the foot of a rib leading to the middle peak.
H P Barcham, A W Bowden, D E Boyd & R J Cunninghame, Jan 1961.

Trident (2068m)

16.14 West Ridge

A 'pleasant scramble' along the crest of the range between the Mueller and Te Naihi Rivers.
T Barcham & A Cunningham, Dec 1950.

Could also be climbed from Stewart Pass at the head of the south branch of Siberia Stream. Although access is possible via Stewart Pass, it is much more difficult than the climb itself. The South Siberia slopes of the pass are steep slabs and bluffs and gully draining it is prone to rockfall.

Dispute (2020m)

16.15

Via snowslopes from the south-east. Grade 1 from the head of Mueller Valley at Lake Dispute.
T Barcham & A Cunningham, Dec 1950.

Dreadful (2030m)

16.16a

The high peak in the centre is climbed via the ridge from the Siberia Valley. There are extensive slabs on this ridge.
J W Aitken, E Miller, J Gillespie & F Wilkinson, Jan 1945.

16.16b

 The south peak has been climbed by traversing from the centre peak.
N Canham & D Fowler, Dec 1958.

Attica (1980m)

16.17

Straightforward from Siberia Saddle.

Doris (2010m)

16.18

Climbed from Governor's Pass at the head of the North Young.
H C Gray, J K Skinner, M R Ellis & A R Craigie, Dec 1948.

Mt Awful (2192m)

If cute was an acceptable word to use to describe a mountain then Mt Awful would be just that. It is a readily accessible peak with good rock as a bonus. It can be approached via the Wilkin Valley and then up Siberia, or up the Young Valley from Makarora.

The Young Valley is probably the best option and has Young Hut as a good base at just above the bush line. Makarora to Young Hut 8–9 hours.

16.19 North Ridge. Grade 1+

From the Siberia Valley climb to the saddle between Doris and Awful, then along the ridge.

J W Aitken, J Gillespie, E Miller, F Wilkinson, Dec 1944.

16.20 East Ridge. Grade 2+

From Young Hut there is a well marked tramping route up onto Gillespie Pass. From here the ridge to Mt Awful is scrambling. There are a couple of rock steps which look steeper than they are before the actual ridge is reached. The climbing on the ridge isn't technically difficult. After a snowfield is climbed there is a section of good solid rock along a knife-edged ridge, which is the trickiest part of the climb and may require a rope and a small rock rack.

East Face

The East Face is a spectacular sweep of good solid rock and is the crowning glory of the Young Valley. There are two routes up the face, both summer rock routes of good quality.

16.21 The Weta Walk. Grade 3 (17)

This nine pitch route climbs out of the snowfield at the bottom left hand side of the face via a four pitch arête at about grade 17. This arête forms the side of a gut which can often be choked with snow or have a waterfall running down it. From the top of this arête head right up a narrow ledge which can have snow on it. This ledge takes you into the middle of the face and into a corner topped by a small roof. A good crack system takes you around the roof and then up into open country.

There is a sting in the tail to this route in the form of a small overlap which is the crux. A piton driven in upside down protected the moves through this overlap, but small cams would probably be better. Two more technical pitches follow and then the face finishes at the summit after a section of scrambling on loose but not horrific rock.

Allan Uren and Clinton Beavan (first ascent of face), Jan 1996.

16.22 A Stitch in Time. Grade 4 (21)

This is a great looking 11 pitch route taking in some well protected climbing in a stunning setting.

16.21

16.22

East Face of Mt Awful, Young Valley in winter conditions.
Allan Uren.

(1) From the snowfield in the middle of the face climb up to a fixed anchor (red tape). 40m, 18.

(2) Step right and up 30m, then angle back left 10m to fixed belay. 40m, 17.

(3) Up 40m to fixed pin, may be difficult to find, then up left to fixed belay. 50m, 19.

(4) Up 2-3m then veer right up seam to fixed belay. 45m, 18.

(5) Up to fixed belay. 45m, 16.

(6) Traverse 8m right along ledge then up to natural belay under roof. 45m, 18.

(7) Step out right onto slab then up 8m to fixed piton. Keep tending right to broad ramp. Follow this left to large ledge and natural belay. 45m, 21. Abseil cord is to your right.

(8) Up and through overlap to abseil sling on ledge. Natural belay. 45m, 18.

Anna Gillooly on the first ascent of *A Stitch in Time*. Young Valley below, Young Hut is on the bushline. *Dave Hiddleston.*

(9) Belay 10m left of abseil sling. Follow obvious crack with a small grass patch and through right facing corner. 51m, 19.

(10) Traverse left finding line of least resistance through broken rock to natural belay. 45m. The abseil sling is to your right.

(11) Tend up and right 15m to abseil cord and walk left 20m to summit.

To get off the face either descend the East Ridge or abseil the route using fixed anchors. Pitch 9 is a 51m abseil onto a broad ledge. Pitch 4 abseil stay hard left, tension on rope for seconder recommended. Pitch 2 abseil trend right. Add a couple of spare pitons.

David Hiddleston & Anna Gillooly, Jan 2000.

Turner (2150m)

16.23

Direct from the Wilkin Valley floor.

D Ball, L W Bruce, A R Craven & M McGuire, Jan 1953.

WATERFALL ICE

Climbing waterfall ice isn't a mainstream sport in New Zealand and this is reflected in the amount of climbable ice, or maybe the amount of climbable ice reflects the lack of climbing. Most of these routes could be described as being obscure and form unreliably but similar things were said about the rock in the area. That isn't to say frozen waterfalls of excellent quality don't exist and more lurk in gloomy backcountry valleys. There have been a few discovered in the lower Matukituki which deserve a mention and even a visit.

Most of the routes above 1600m and in the shade are reliable and form thick and strong ice. In certain weather conditions, that is during early winter when there is an inversion, some interesting flows have formed below this altitude. These should be approached with a deep suspicion especially if the sun is out. There is even a wandering waterfall up the West Matukituki near the Otago Boys High School lodge, which flows down to the valley floor and freezes in some winters. Maybe you'll be the one lucky enough to find it in condition.

Grading

The North American system of grading waterfall ice has been loosely adopted for these flows, all care and no responsibility. It is a single number like the NZ alpine system but differs in that the number is generally just a technical grade and doesn't take into account length or seriousness, like a rock grade. The number is preceded by WI meaning water ice. These grades are also loose as they have only seen one ascent.

Gear

A rack of seven to eight ice screws and a couple of snow stakes. Short, cut down snowstakes, like a sawn off shotgun, can come in handy in less than perfect ice. Rock gear isn't generally of any use but a selection of pitons might come in handy. If available drive-in, screw-out ice screws, *Snargs* that is, are brilliant for driving into frozen turf. Snowstakes work in a similar way and can be driven into the rotten rock and crevices.

The climbs

Black Peak (2289m)

On the South East Face of Black peak are two quality routes. Underneath the summit snowfield there is a line of bluffs with a ramp running from right to left underneath them. The routes are on these bluffs. These lines can be viewed from the Mt Aspiring lookout at the Treble Cone Ski Area. This is a wild place to climb and has a feeling more akin to climbing in the greater Alps. To get to these lines you can use the routes described in the Black Peak lower valley section or a helicopter can be used for an express lift from Charlie Ewing at Cattle Flat station.

LEFT. Clinton Beavan in the Rainbow Stream Cirque, winter 1996.
Allan Uren.

The Straight Jacket Fits (WI 3) 150m

This route climbs out of a small alcove at the top of the line of bluffs. The first pitch is the steepest. Above this a few laid back pitches lead up a gully to the snow field.

Allan Uren, August 1993.

Huge (WI 5) 200m

When you know where to look this flow can be seen from Wanaka. It is contained in a gully and once again the steepest section is at the bottom. On the first ascent the icicles were formed up in steps with a small overhang to be surmounted. The pitches are four long ones and end at the snow-field. Both of these routes are relatively safe from avalanches. However the ramp to access them should be treated with kid gloves.

Dave Vass & Allan Uren, August 1993.

South side of Black Peak

There is an expansive crag of ice near the bottom of the South Face of Black Peak. It is on a line of bluffs facing east. There isn't a lot of information on this ice as only a few ascents have been made, but it looks like the whole spectrum from mellow to mental is covered.

Dave Langrish attempting a new route, Black Peak. Winter 1999.
Allan Uren.

Black Peak ice routes.
A - Huge
B - The Staight Jacket Fits
C - Access ramp
Allan Uren.

Niger Peak (2023m)

Cardrona Cafe Girls (WI 2) 100m

This route is on the South side of Niger Peak above the Matuktuki Station, R Ewing's property and can be seen from the Matukituki road, on a line of bluffs overlooking the gorge of Niger Stream. It takes about three hours to reach the base of the route via a sheep track on the true right of Niger Stream. This track wends its way under a line of bluffs and comes out above the gorge. Cross the stream and head up and through scrappy bush to reach the bottom of the route. The alpine scrub getting to the bottom of the route is jungle like and time consuming.

Cardrona Cafe Girls is the right hand line and is about two pitches in length. The crux is at half height and is a small vertical step. If this is wet and dripping a detour can be made out right via an interesting section of mixed frozen tussock and blobs of ice. The slopes above appear to be active avalanche zones. If there is any doubt about stability perhaps rappeling the route would be a good idea. There is good bouldering and a small beautiful chandelier in the clearing above the stream gorge.

Allan Uren, July 1991.

South East side of Niger Peak, out of
Leaping Burn. Route is *Cardrona Café
Girls* (WI 2) 100m.
Allan Uren.

Fog Peak (2240m)
HMH (WI 4/5) 100m

This stunning flow is easily reached using a helicopter and then skiing out down the Leaping Burn. It is at the head of the East Branch of the Polnoon Burn on the south eastern slopes of Fog Peak. The name is in recognition of the Heli ski guides who passed on the location of this classic line.

The first pitch ends after climbing 80 degree stepped ice, in an ice cave large enough to shelter four people. The second pitch erupts out of the cave and onto a 40m pillar. If the left hand side is climbed then the grade is WI 3+ on 85 degree stepped ice. If the right side is clung to then vertical grade 5 climbing could be expected. On the first ascent the left hand side was climbed. *Dave Vass, Allan Uren and Rachel Brown, Sept 1996.*

➠ Another water ice crag with easy access and fine climbing is to be found over at Wye Creek behind the Remarkables Ski Area.

Climber

Belay Cave

HMH (WI4) 100m, Fog Peak, in winter, 1995. Paul Scaife.

INDEX

Page numbers are in plain type,
photograph references are in semi-bold.

SERVICE LISTINGS

Guiding Companies

Adventure Consultants Wanaka
Phone **03 443-8711** Fax **03 443-8733**
Email **info@adventure.co.nz**
Web **www.adventure.co.nz**

Mount Aspiring Guides Wanaka
Phone **03 443-9422**
Email **aspguide@xtra.co.nz**
Web **www.mtaspiringguides.co.nz**

Mountain Recreation Ltd Wanaka
Phone **03 443-7330**
Email **mountainrec@mountainrec.co.nz**
Web **www.mountainrec.co.nz**

Mountain Works Queenstown
Freephone **0508 SUMMIT** Phone **03 442-7329** Mobile **021 220-5950**
Email **mtnworks@queenstown.co.nz**
Web **www.mountainworks.co.nz**

Alpine Guides (Aoraki) Ltd Mt Cook
Phone **03 435-1834** Fax **03 435-1898**
Email **mtcook@alpineguides.co.nz**
Web **www.alpineguides.co.nz**

Southern Alps Guiding Twizel-Mt Cook
Phone **03 435-0890** Fax **03 326-7518**
Email **charles@outside.co.nz**
Web **www.mtcook.com**

126

SERVICE LISTINGS

Air Services

Aspiring Helicopters Ltd Wanaka
Phone **03 443-7152** Mobile **025 744-999** Fax **03 443-7102**
Email **charlie.mel@xtra.co.nz**

Southern Alps Air Ltd Wanaka
Phone **03 443-8666**

Wanaka Helicopters Wanaka
Phone **03 443-1085 anytime** Fax **03 443-1086**
Email **info@heliflights.co.nz** Web **www.heliflights.co.nz**

Retailers

Bivouac Outoor
76 Cashel Mall, Christchurch
171 George Street, Dunedin
Phone **0800 BIVOUAC** (248682)

Camp NZ mail order New Plymouth
Phone **06 758-7144** Fax **06 757-8602**
Address **PO Box 849, New Plymouth**

Element Queenstown
Phone **03 442-2445**
Address **Remarkables Park, Frankton**

Mountain Designs
654 Colombo St, Christchurch 03 377-8522
28 Halifax St, Nelson 03 548-8208
51 Shotover St, Queenstown Opening Soon

127

The NZAC is New Zealand's leading publisher and distributor of climbing and backcountry guidebooks.

Contact the National Office for our latest stocklist and prices or check out our website:

www.alpineclub.org.nz

Phone 03 377 7595
Fax 03 377 7594
E-mail publications@alpineclub.org.nz

Back cover: Clockwise from top left: Keas and Colin Todd Hut. *Colin Monteath/Hedgehog House*. Illusory telephoto shot of the South West Ridge of Mount Aspiring from Cascade Saddle. *Colin Monteath/ Hedgehog House*. Dave Vass on lead during an attempt on a direct line, South East Face of Pope's Nose, winter 1998. Kerie Carson in the upper Wilkin Valley. *Allan Uren*.